The City Commute

The City Commute

The Art & Science of Life's Most Tedious Journey

The City Commute

Copyright © 2020 by Peter Welch

All rights reserved. This book or any portion thereof may not be reproduced or used in any manner whatsoever without the express written permission of the publisher except for the use of brief quotations in a book review.

Printed in the United States of America

First Printing: December 2020

ISBN: 978-0-9853181-9-2

12by3 Press
P.O. Box 110037
263 South 4th St.
Brooklyn, NY 11211-9997

www.12by3.com

In loving memory of my commute

HOW TO USE THIS BOOK

There are two hundred standard working days per year in the continental United States, assuming two weeks of vacation, and ignoring the unlikely event that an employer respects federal holidays. This is a well-known travesty built on a variety of mechanisms, including, but not limited to, free-market capitalism, economically gated education, and Ayn Rand. The purpose of this book is not to untangle this situation. Nor is it to assist in the march between the end of parental support and the degradations of age deemed sufficient to render a person insufficiently exploitable.

Those two hundred days contain an average of four hundred journeys, known to English speakers as commutes. Navigating these hundreds of hours of travel is a major component of most workers' lives, yet rarely contemplated to any depth.

Within the following pages are one hundred meditations on the theory and practice of commuting. It was supposed to be two hundred, to reflect the full year of working days, but the author had to get on with his life. Hence, it is recommended to engage with only two or three chapters a week, to better ponder the intricacies of each subject.

Since nobody is going to do that and this whole book can probably be finished in three hours, another possibility: upon finishing, sign it, note down where you are, and leave it there for the next commuter, that the book may make its own journey. This may prove difficult with digital editions; it is left as an exercise for the reader.

A final note on the content: The majority of it concerns the city, but the overarching theories can be applied to any environment. A city is but a locus of commerce within a broader context, and the author has endeavored to reflect this gestalt within the manuscript.

PRIMARY AND SECONDARY PRINCIPLES

The principles of commuting comprise an art like any other. They are general guides to an ongoing process, applicable to the immediate situation, as well as to the practice as a whole, and to the shaping of a life's work in the form.

The principle of least effort is the primary principle, guiding the commuter to be like water: to be still when possible, and flow smoothly around obstacles when they arise.

The secondary principles are derived from the primary: the principle of shortest path and the principle of minimal friction. Shortest path merely directs the commuter to cut all corners and seek the straightest road. Minimal friction dictates avoiding confrontation and collision and striving to appear as though nothing is in the way.

In practicing these principles, the commute shortens and eases. Those of the higher ranks will barely seem to travel. One who truly masters of the art of commuting will not commute at all. Or they shall own a helicopter.

MORNING

Sleep has been a tricky judgment call since the dawn of the electric age. Locked in dim offices and dimmer homes, our rhythms of light are dependent on switches, the long history of culture and genetics be damned.

With the constancy of our nearest star belied by the intimate domination of artificial suns, the only sure measure of the day is the workday. Thus, the morning is no longer the dawn, but the approach of an hour marked as a numeral between 7 and 10-ish.

Perhaps the notion of "morning person" existed prior to the 1800s. More likely, predilections toward waking hours were labeled upstanding and degenerate, or perhaps commoner and noble in the same order. Regardless, the ability to fall asleep at a desk without undue risk of setting the desk on fire made for all manner of potentially profitable schedules.

Much has been said of nightwalkers versus daywalkers, and much of what has been said is pointless speculation over tiny sample sizes and spurious correlation. If, in fact, creative people stay up later and successful people wake up earlier, the proper response is not to promote a sleep schedule, but to quickly and earnestly reevaluate what creativity and success mean, because they have clearly become petty notions to be marked on the Y axis of a scatterplot.

Commuting offers a simpler evaluation of the schedule. The nightwalker will have turned the morning into the automatic execution of the necessary motions. They have little time, less so with each punch of the snooze button. Their mornings are groggy; pray they don't need to operate heavy machinery. Yet their nights strike them as endless opportunity, and their commute home is of little consequence, no matter its hour.

The daywalker's hours of opportunity are in the dawn, long before they need to ready themselves for mortal commute. Though time is restricted to the hours between alarm and door, the time is peaceful, for consciousness—the great hurdle of the morning—has been achieved. The necessary preparations can be attended to with calm deliberation, and the mind is fresh to accomplish leisure or hobby before facing the world. Their nights are another matter: To be a daywalker is to hurry home with the setting sun and be sure to feed, wash, brush, and relax, with an urgency not classically compatible with relaxation or attentive bodily maintenance.

Most fall into a pattern without any notable decisions. Should agency be applied to the situation, the only true difference is that it's easier to drink as a nightwalker, and easier to smoke weed as a daywalker. Cocaine goes both ways.

THE DEPARTURE PARADOX

When flying, it is best to schedule a departure at the airport as early as possible. Planes leaving at six or seven in the morning tend to be less crowded, and to leave on time, because delays and problems haven't had time to stack up, and the kind of people who schedule early flights are also the kind of people who get there on time, so on a lucky day, morning planes have even been known to leave before their scheduled time.

Subways display similar behavior, leading to the Departure Paradox, which states that if a commute begins at a time and place on a subway line where the trains can no longer absorb the rush-hour traffic, it does not matter what time the commute is begun during the hour of the rush. For instance, given a rush hour between 8:15 and 9:15, both the person who departs at 8:16 and the person who departs at 9:14 will arrive at their destination sometime between 9:30 and 9:45.

Once the traffic volume reaches critical density, problems start piling up. A train is no good to a commuter if can't be boarded, but frustrated commuters will try anyway, thus delaying the trains, thus creating more trains with too many people, etc. As the trains get fuller, probability demands that someone will have a medical emergency and pass out at a major station. Delays multiply and feed back, and a twenty-minute train ride rapidly, so to speak, becomes an hour long. This process is already in full swing by 8:30, and slowly winds down, ending by 9:30, so the later the hour is broached, the shorter the trip is likely to be.

CROSS WHEN . . .

Grid navigation demands the eternal debate: Cross when you can? Or cross when you have to?

Given a grid laden with streetlights, this may appear to be a non-question, as the will is impeded by the illuminated instructions, but the core philosophy of crossing informs the actions taken in the yellow and blinking red wiggle rooms allotted human agency within this structure, even dismissing the anarchic jaywalkers and lightrunners. Is it worth it to race across an avenue, trusting the lingering blink of a red hand and the better natures of automobile navigators? Or is it better to accept fate and alter trajectory when providence allows?

At first glance, the principle of least friction suggests cross when you have to, as this situation, written in streetlight, implies an easy and traffic-mandated means of progress. Yet cross when you can certainly appears to adhere to the principle of shortest path. This ostensibly simple debate appears to be the beginning of a schism!

But it is not. The true theory of crossing is a corollary of both principles, and it is this: cross as to minimize future stops.

Assuming a destination northwest of a current location, the commuter must move north and west along the straight lines of the grid, and when given a choice, always move in the direction along which there is a greater distance to travel. If the destination is two blocks west and ten blocks north, every decision should involve northward travel until the destination is two blocks north, at which point it doesn't matter. Adhering to this preference increases the odds that there will always be continued movement when there is no option, for once there is only a single axis of travel, the commuter will have no choice but to stop at every red light.

When the rules appear in conflict, there is often a second-degree principle derivable from the core precepts. In this case, it is the principle of continual motion. This principle in part follows from least friction, in that changes in speed increase friction, but is not completely derivable, because changes in direction also increase friction, so the calculation must be buttressed by using shortest path. Since the path on an ideal grid is always the same length, simply substitute time for distance, and the answer is clear.

FIELD NOTES: SOCIALIZING

Once, in some misguided attempt to be healthier, I forwent my morning coffee and cigarette until after I'd braved the subway. Or I got up late and didn't have time to make coffee, and I can't smoke a cigarette until I'm working through my first cup. One of those.

The mind of a pack-a-day smoker prior to the first cigarette is like superheated water. Placid crystal until the slightest impurity is introduced, whereupon it boils explosively. By the time I left the apartment, I'd already snapped once trying to put on a wool sweater that was about a size and a half too small. I spent the fifteen-minute walk trying to reclaim my mental purity for the first train.

Despite the initial ten-minute wait, I didn't even bother trying to get on the first train, already packed beyond any sensible safety regulation. During this further delay, a close friend of mine wandered by and took out his headphones to say, "Are you one of those people who likes to chat with their friends on the train in the morning?"

"Well, sometimes, but I haven't had coffee," I tried to say, though it came out closer to, "Well vshwom bu haven'ts coffshe."

He nodded and put his headphones back in. "Great, I'm going to stand a ways down."

Relieved, I managed to get on the second train. It was crowded, and quiet.

WAITING

There is no better example of existential futility than waiting for public transportation. Anger itself becomes muted on the subway platform during a long wait, because there's nothing to be angry at. Even a bus has a visible driver who can receive an angry glance; a train might have a head sticking out of a window, but probably not the head responsible for navigation. There's just an anonymous tube of uncertain ETA. Until it does show up, there's nothing to be done.

Commuters crane their necks to see another two feet into the distance, looking for a bus or taxi or train, and it is valid to wonder why they bother. It will never make the bus come faster. It is tempting to compare them to sports fans believing they can contribute to a game through a television, but the truth is people want to see the headlights at the soonest possible moment, because the fear that this time it will never come is the creeping dread the ego must disprove.

Once this fear is acknowledged, the logical actions fall into place automatically: stop looking, turn up the headphones, read a book, and make no effort to notice the approach of the vessel until it arrives. Looking down subway tunnels is pointless anyway, because in most subterranean stations, the breeze from the oncoming train precedes all other sensory evidence.

But something about being underground makes it worse. The idea that a train might never come is sister to the fear that everything not seen might not exist at all, and there's not much to see in a subway station. After half an hour, the thought begins to tug in the basement of the brain: Maybe this is all there is. A walkway filled with strangers, next to a tunnel leading into darkness in both directions. Darkness that may or may not contain trains.

STANDING ON THE PLATFORM

There are two elements to platform position: longitudinal and latitudinal. The longitudinal position is determined by the optimal point to exit the train upon reaching the destination. However, this positioning must take into account the popularity of the desired exit, which will inform the population density near that position on the train. Additionally, there are features of the platform that may decrease the desirability of the location, including, but not limited to, airflow in the given station, proximity to the station entrance, and whether the position is under the grating on a busy street. Though it may seem obvious that the openings above the platforms correspond to the gratings on the street above the stations, it is rarely acknowledged or considered until after the errant bit of discarded trash bounces its way onto the shoulder of an unlucky commuter.

The latitudinal position is measured as distance from the track. Though it varies from city to city, there are, for each side of the track, an average of three lanes on the platform: track, aisle, and wall. Wall position is ideal; without even taking into account back support, the wall position minimizes obstruction—as all nonhuman obstruction is already wall-side—and maximizes safety. Track position is acceptable, but be aware that this reduces the distance between commuting and death to one dizzy spell or one crazy person, and these are both abundant in major cities, especially in the summer. It is also more obstructive than wall position, as the lane may need to be used to accommodate bidirectional traffic during peak travel hours. It is more acceptable—and safer—when there is a supporting beam by the track. Indeed, when there are two tracks bordering the platform, trackside beam becomes an optimal latitudinal position, in the absence of a wall.

Do not wait in the aisle. Standing in the aisle is ontologically indistinguishable from being a jackass. If the reader does not understand why this is so, the reader is the worst kind of jackass.

THE OBSTACLE

The obstacle is always an irritation, but, viewed as simply an obstacle, deserves no particular emotional energy, when the energy can be better put toward navigation. However, it is impossible not to occasionally recognize an obstacle as human, and if no effort is made to achieve this recognition consciously, it will always surface at the crest of a negative emotional tide.

The cumulative effect of only engaging with the reality of Otherness while experiencing distress is to degrade the semiotic distinction between obstacle and Other. Otherness is by its nature imbued with emotional obstructions; when the very concept of Other is conflated with personal difficulty, those inherent obstructions become all but impassable. The mere concept of other people becomes a source of the very distress eroding the commuter's ability to deal with them in an emotionally neutral and healthy space.

Worse, the recognition of this pattern of reinforcement does not preclude its continuance. It might make it worse. To think something anathema to a belief system is to train the mind to be comfortable with internal dissonance. Indeed, further betrayals of the self's conscientious compass alleviate guilt of past betrayals, and it becomes a soothing routine to indulge in hateful thought, in much the same way that addiction requires the mind to provide an explanatory framework immune to better nature.

This addiction to contempt is easy to cultivate because it is comprised solely of distressing external stimulus (the Other barring the way) and soothing internal stimulus (justification for contempt) in an otherwise neutral setting of communal indifference. Furthermore, there is no foreseeable end to the true Asshole Others who seem to provide empirical support for the increasing rejection of external humanity. At the end of this collapsing distinction between obstacle and Other lies righteous hatred, the most inhumane facet of humanity.

Sadly, there is no simple method for escaping this cycle, nor is there a method of transmuting it into something obviously and personally beneficial to the average commuter. The only way to escape it is to recognize, fully, and to the detriment of the ego, that this demonization of the Other-as-obstacle is impotent, and a waste of thought. Then, atop this humiliation, it is necessary to make the conscious effort to reframe the moment of recognizing the obstacle as another human. Instead of applying the aspect of obstruction to the Other, apply the unknown story of a commuter navigating all-too-familiar obstructions. With practice, it may be possible to once again see them as human.

FIELD NOTES: 4/5/6

I've ridden a lot of trains at rush hour in NYC. The least crowded was the PATH to Jersey, because I was taking it in reverse, since nobody actually lives in Brooklyn and works in Jersey. I regularly had an entire car to myself. The ads were the best part: one advertised condos in Hoboken by pointing out that if you live on the Jersey waterfront, you get to look at the Manhattan skyline, whereas if you live in Manhattan, you have to look at Jersey. They had a point. Another ad proclaimed, "Have you talked to your kids about drugs? Because their friends are." The grammatical problems with these two sentences made me grind my teeth for a year.

The exact opposite of this advertising-meditation commute was taking the 4/5/6 uptown from 14th Street at nine in the morning. I've never seen anything like it outside of dystopian-future cinema. A lucky day involved getting down the stairs and making the third train. Often, there was a line just to get to the head of the stairs, and you could spend five minutes on them before you got to the platform below. When there was room for them, MTA officials would move people around and clear entrances with flashlights and shouting. The platform was often past the tipping point long before I arrived.

People snapped on a regular basis. I witnessed the most impotent fight of all time as two men yelled at each other over the impenetrable press of people between them, unable even to make a threatening gesture because their hands were pinned to their sides.

The 4/5/6 at 14th is also the loudest of all train stops, reaching 106 decibels, which starts causing hearing damage after thirty seconds. The screeching achieved by every single train is equivalent to having headphones comprised of two hungry babies. People who just say, "Gimme a second," into their cell phones and don't blink when multiple ambulances go by still flinch when a slow 6 train pulls into 14th Street.

If you're not from the city, the 4/5/6 is the green line on the subway map. This is your only warning.

COFFEE ACQUIREMENT

Service-industry employees do not pretend to like customers in Manhattan. This is part of the service they provide. The commuting horde's component members generally recognize this: The person behind the counter isn't interested in getting to know an individual, but the coldness of that shoulder is mediated by the fact that they weren't interested in the three individuals that came before. Instead, they cranked through everyone's orders and got everybody back out into the fray as quickly as possible. Pit crews don't lean in the window and ask how the driver's day is going. Manhattan coffeeslingers don't either, and for the same reasons.

This is not to say there is no hope of a professional relationship with morning energy providers. The basic duties on the customer's side of the transaction are preparedness and acceptance. Preparedness consists of having means of payment ready before it is time to order and knowing what that order will be before arriving at the register. It seems simple enough, but all have, in moments of distraction, encountered the moment of payment as an unexpected shock. This is an acceptable mistake as long as it is not a common one.

Acceptance is harder. Do not expect a genuine session of social call-and-response. They may inquire after the quality of the day, but they do not want to know and will not listen if told. Smiling is acceptable, flirting is not; this isn't a restaurant. Do not order things that do not exist. Leave the register as soon as the transaction is complete; there are other places to return means of payment to its container. Do not give exact change unless it is a small amount and prepared beforehand. A professional money handler can find sixty-two cents far more expediently than any amateur consumer can find thirty-eight. In fact, most can dispense sixty-two cents faster than they can put away an unsorted handful of dimes and pennies.

Those who follow these principles unfailingly at a regular location begin to stand out among customers, and will start to find their drinks prepared before they reach the register. It may even cost less. The entire transaction can be reduced to eye contact and a thank-you. They may genuinely want to know how your day is going, in which case it is acceptable to respond with one sentence of up to twenty words.

THE ZIPPER

At no place is the human capacity for cooperation better evinced than the paved delta that empties into the Holland Tunnel. It can take hours to reach the last few merging lanes that lead to the tunnel under the bodies at the bottom of the river between Manhattan and New Jersey. Hours of counting the streetlight cycles, trying not to block the box, watching delivery trucks move an inch a minute, and yet: When all the tired and angry drivers reach the merging lanes, they merge perfectly, each one of them respecting the turn-based system that saves them all from the road-rage slaughter that will ensue the day one of them doesn't.

It's a simple thing. Given two lanes becoming one, one car from the left goes, one car from the right goes. Wait your turn, take your turn. Even in one of the most congested places on Earth, crowded with vehicles designed to strip away the checks and balances of human nature, driven by people who have ignored—out of spite or obliviousness—every order relayed by a thousand street signs and a dozen screaming pedestrians: The zipper is respected by law and perfectly executed by every attendant brain. Here, they understand the greater good.

So it is odd that the zipper often fails at subway turnstiles. Surely empathy would be stronger when faced with human forms, and the zipper more firmly followed. Alas, it is the irony of empathy that it is most firmly crushed when it is most needed. Quick changes for optimal pathfinding, executed with insufficient information, create a jagged strainer. There is always a desperate trickle of ingress looking for holes in the exodus, and its meaningless attempts to combat the outflow create last-minute second-guesses in the well-meaning arrivals so close, so very close to the freedom of the streets.

It's a tricky moment. One person has to look another person in the face, or at least the mid-torso, and decide between the momentary happiness of a recognized human in front of them, and the momentary happiness of the three or more people behind them. All participants may be armed.

Thus the failure of empathy is twofold. In its rejection, some are blocked from their destination. In its acceptance, many are delayed in their escape.

THE TIPPING POINT

The tipping point on the New York subway is when commuters go from trying to make room to holding their ground. There is no more room, and any room conceded to new bodies is given by the squeezing and contorting of existing bodies. In this situation, if the commuter does not hold their square foot of ground, they will be bent over someone who's hanging off the overhead handrail trying not to shove their genitalia in the face of someone lucky enough to have a seat. Bags are between the commuter's feet at this point, and any further loss of ground could mean losing a bag. It will also be impossible to make sure a wallet is still in its appropriate pocket without copping a feel from whomever is pressed against said pocket. In this quiet mosh pit, elbows start to tighten out of necessity, and the desperate calm begins to fray.

All motion after the tipping point is equal parts tango and yoga in slow motion, bags retrieved in synchronized dips, exit paths discovered by touch and twitch, and tempers managed by extreme acts of will.

FIELD NOTES: DRIZZLE

When commuting to work from my girlfriend's apartment, my morning ritual involves a small cup of extremely expensive coffee from a small shop three blocks north of her building. It takes two or three minutes to make, because it's brewed a cup at a time and because it wouldn't be a luxury item if it were expedient. Once I have my coffee, I sit on the step of a store a couple of doors down and smoke. This store has been under construction or deconstruction for a year or more, so I don't think anybody minds. This whole process takes about ten minutes, after which I do the ten-minute walk from the shop step to my office.

Not long ago, these first ten minutes happened to be the ten minutes the sky took to turn from sunny and clear to gray and beginning to rain.

Actual rain changes the walking dynamic into a scurrying maze of death and hate, but pre-rain drizzle has the less dramatic effect of magnifying preexisting commuter habits. Fast walkers lengthen their strides, opportunists break into dashes more frequently, the lost sheep look a little more lost as they eye the sky. A few people already have umbrellas up. The people who have to work outside and don't care about anything continue to not care, but except for them, the pace of the street ratchets up a couple of cranks as everyone tries to shave off a few of the minutes between them and their target door.

Overall, it worked out well for me. The drizzle dispersed the mini-clusters of people looking over stolen or knockoff goods along Hester Street and brought the amblers up to speedwalker status. For some reason the lost sheep seemed to have wandered their way into another time frame: One woman took a full thirty seconds to traverse the S curve she was following in front of a delivery truck trying to make a right turn, and a man who couldn't have been over five feet tall managed to block an otherwise unobstructed sidewalk with a cane and a single plastic bag. I wondered if this was some kind of obscure martial art.

The only things that become more dangerous in pre-rain conditions are the bicycles. Cyclists already eschew law and order in favor of speed, and when the rain is coming, the space reserved for their sense of superiority is annexed by their already amply housed sense of entitlement. Fortunately, they remain a bigger danger to themselves than anyone else, but it's important to stay out of the bike lanes.

I got to work with only a light moistening, which I dried off with the company shirt somebody ordered without asking anybody what size they wore. The rain stopped two minutes later.

UNCERTAINTY

Careful sidewalk navigation requires an understanding of the uncertainty principle of pedestrian velocity.

Briefly stated: The more rapid the forward motion of a pedestrian object, the less certain one can be of its future position, and the slower the forward motion of said object, the less certain one can be of its future direction.

Fortunately, there are statistical measures that apply. The higher the speed, the narrower the cone of effect, so once determined, there is only a 10 percent chance that the mover will exit that cone, and the event requiring the exit will invariably signal the exit and allow for evasive maneuvers, unless one happens to be the event.

The more dangerous pedestrian by far is the one failing to pedest, for they can strike out in any direction without warning. In many cases, a small drifting motion will indicate the pedestrian's intent to exit the conversation they are currently in with either another mostly still pedestrian or an eConversant; this will give approximately a meter-radius semicircle of *zona peligrosa* to avoid, as the drifting body will invariably turn suddenly in the direction of its desired future motion, moving through an arc of space its navigational senses have failed to check for obstacles. This drifting motion is referred to as *cepit oblivio signum*, and can be easily observed and prepared for with minimal practice.

Those with no indication of future direction present a danger that is blessedly rare, but one that cannot be predicted, and thus cannot be prepared for. The only defense is to note that the *zona* is still approximately one meter, and it behooves one to listen for a destination being discussed and to note the angle of the line between it and the unmoving speaker.

ELEVATE

In many jobs, the final element of the commute is an elevator. It is a peculiar moment. The commuter has done all that can be done: planned the route, navigated road and walkway, acquired necessary sustenance, and, above all, survived until reaching the elevator. At this point, they are mechanically put at the mercy of every other commuter with whom they share building and schedule.

Hidden in a column of steel and hopefully unyielding cable, the elevator's rise and fall is dictated by base speed, stops, held doors, and delivery persons gaming the system by sending the elevator up two floors so they can catch it on the way down. All this is reduced to a single inscrutable number, and perhaps an arrow, communicating little more than distance to the hungry eyes of the stilled commuter.

This implacable opponent is met at the very moment the commuter must shed their optimization instincts and remember their humanity. Early morning elevator talk is a practice run, as the trapped minds reorient toward social-bonding rituals, after twenty to ninety minutes of social-avoidance necessities. It is awkward, halting, yet marked by eagerness as the mind seeks connection at its most vulnerable public moment of the day. We reach for humanity shyly, after so thoroughly rejecting it. Faced with the cold clockwork of the unknowable elevator, we are reminded that there are more insurmountable obstacles than one another.

BAGGAGE

Some basic rules of weapons training are to make the weapon an extension of the body, and to know where it is and what it is doing at all times. This sort of training should be mandatory for anybody navigating a city.

There are two primary modes of carrying a bag. For subway navigation, it can be held at the side, so it takes up the minimum amount of radial space and can be quickly moved in front of or behind the body when the available corridors of motion start to constrict.

At street level, if the foot traffic isn't too dense, it can go over the shoulder, which is comfortable, but requires being aware that the shoulder is now extruding eight inches farther behind and three or four inches farther to the right of the body. This may seem a small amount, but navigation in the commercial districts of Manhattan during the day is often a matter of inches. A sudden twist of the torso could knock a fellow commuter to the ground, so it is important to account for this extended space consumption when calculating safe turns and passings.

Most fail to expand their kinetic awareness when encumbered with even their daily baggage. This is most often demonstrated by the standing spin, wherein a person with a bag of some kind is talking to someone, then suddenly needs to look in another direction, so they do a full turn and manage to block an entire sidewalk, often hitting a passerby with their bag in the process. The spinner simply doesn't understand that they are consuming space outside their body.

Simply put: You are what you carry.

FIELD NOTES: OBITS

If I had died on the morning of October 14, 2009, in the manner I suspected I might, this is what my obituary would have said:

"Peter Welch was struck and killed by a bacon delivery truck while crossing Hester Street in Chinatown. He died as he lived."

KNEE JERK

Controlling anger is vital to successful navigation. Anger tenses the muscles, reducing fluid movement and inviting cramping. Tiny affronts to decency can compound quickly, and it is best to brush them off as the casual accidents and oblivious acts that they are.

In a large enough community, dehumanization is inevitable. The novice considers every other human as a fully realized being, thus scripts emotional relationships, assuming measures of attention and recognition from the Other that do not exist. Assuming this attention, they react as their own nature dictates, and become reactive in their commuting behavior in the hopes of affirming their self-image in the mind of the Other, not realizing the Other's mind rarely considers them more than a vague shape between them and the door.

The practiced commuter has let go of such imagined relationships. Other persons are now people; the trees have become the forest, and the forest is dark. Fellow commuters are no longer fellows, but erratic and dangerous obstacles to be dodged and defeated for the singular purpose of movement.

The master commuter realizes they are one of the trees, and the harmony of the forest is in each tree finding its own water and light amid many others much like itself. Recognition of other people as fellows returns, but is not burdened with personal, ego-driven connections: It is the recognition of many personal intents weaving through one another based on a handful of personal principles and desires, creating a flow that can be navigated by focusing on the awareness of oneself within the flow.

Thus in mastery can the emotional friction of commuting be mitigated with the abstraction of the many into one.

Until one of the intents or people or trees or whatever starts ramming his knees into your back on the stairs because he saw a train pull in and decided the well-being of the people in front of him were secondary to the thirty seconds he could save by getting to his optimal subway car. Here, the principles of commuting are unclear on whether it is best to let this pass, despite having to lunge for the railing to avoid falling down the stairs, or to turn and grab the owner of the knees, hurl him to the floor, and punch him repeatedly in the dick while screaming, "WAS IT WORTH IT FUCKSTICK? NOT GONNA MAKE YOUR FUCKING TRAIN NOW, ARE YA?"

Unfortunately, in the only recorded instance of this event, the assaulting party ducked through an opening in traffic, and the assaulted commuter was unable to locate him in the train, so the question must remain unanswered.

There are as many reasons for the failure to maintain communal momentum as there are pigeons in Venice. Physical ailment by accident or age are common, and no human should judge harshly their own future; indeed, when trapped behind such a cause of stillness, a student of movement should take the moment to contemplate the reasons for their journey through time and space.

Confusion, for all the sighs and *tsk*s it generates, is understandable, particularly in any system of public works transporting any notable number of persons. The morally superior act, when faced with the slowness that grows from confusion, is to dispel the confusion with aid, thus dispersing greater knowledge into the commuter milieu.

Distraction is a less forgivable cause of slowness, albeit a common one. Tragically, there is little to do with the distracted that does not violate the principle of least friction, but if a practitioner does have a modicum of the mythical Time to Spare, it may be spent in an effort to remind a distracted person of the thin and narrowing line between life and death.

The larger the nonmartial group, the slower it moves, for two reasons: Groups incur the social costs of signaling and acknowledgment, which constitute distraction, and a group may only move as quickly as its slowest member. In groups larger than four, it has been mathematically proven that this slowest member is a nervous Frenchman texting with his wife, so when faced with a group of five or more, elaborate detours are advisable.

All of these slowings are the unavoidable price of motion among mammals. But there is one action anathema to the practice of commuting: the slowboater.

Slowboaters are not slow because they are enfeebled, confused, or distracted. Slowboaters do not obfuscate exits because they have friends; indeed, it is evident that they do not. Slowboaters drag their heels across roads and through turnstiles, sometimes coming to complete stops in the middle of desperate commuting hoards. They do it to demonstrate that they do not care about other people. They do it to prop up identities savaged by failure or success, craving a challenge to fill the strip-mall parking lots where their hearts should be. Dare one express the hate that slowboaters deserve so completely, they take false umbrage at the suggestion that their kingdoms of contempt should be challenged by peasants, and cast their accuser as the villain in their solipsistic craving for victimhood.

There is no appropriate action to be taken against the slowboater, for action is what they desire, and will only fuel them. If they are unavoidable, the less-than-optimal approach is to move them aside like an object and ignore their inevitable and protracted protests. They will shout at you, they will attempt to demean you, to spur you into becoming an aggressor who can briefly outshine the sad aggression of their own lives, and you must not bite.

Unless you have a taser. Then you should tase the fucker.

BLIND SPOT

After ignition, gas pedal, break, and the mirrors that are supposed to be checked every eight seconds that nobody checks more than once every five minutes, checking the blind spot is one of the fundamentals of driving.

The ludicrousness of this activity should not be lost on the casual driver. There is no excuse for blind spots, even with the optical reflective technology of 1950, yet there they lie, just a few feet behind the driver's seat. Drivers of a certain age check their blind spots prior to any lateral movement of their speeding murder machine. Drivers who do not check their blind spots do not reach a certain age, or, if they do, are no longer drivers.

When driving, it is both a basic principle of safety to check the blind spot for other drivers, and a basic principle of etiquette to not be in another driver's blind spot. To not be in another's blind spot while driving is only a principle of etiquette because it is marginally safe to assume the fellow driver will in fact check their blind spot, due to safety concerns.

In pedestrian traffic, the safety and etiquette concerns are reversed. Given the ability of a slow-moving human to injure anything within three feet of its center of gravity without warning or even intent, it is logically superior to avoid that sphere of danger at most costs. Meanwhile, the forward pedestrian should check their blind spot before executing the potentially dangerous lateral movement.

The tragedy is that few leg-centric commuters check their blind spots. Perhaps underestimating the potential danger inherent to nonautomotive means of transit, a pedestrian human body oft flails through changes in velocity with little to no inclination to visually clear the field of their spasmodic motion.

In automotive transit, we plead with newcomers to understand their potential to cause death. Would that we pleaded as desperately with the unadorned human to understand their potential to cause pain.

SEASONS

Be they wet or dry, cold or hot, short or long, planting or harvest, sunless or nightless, or covered in slowly graying piles of ice, a season and its accompanying weather are, and have always been, the basic common unit of experience for all creatures and conversation.

For a bushel of millennia, the minute changes of seasonal temperature and habit were of vital import to the continuation of the species. Festivals and rituals of all sorts are nailed to rough estimations of meaningful changes in the amount of sunlight and precipitation. In these moments resides our genuflection to the motions of the Earth and sun, for where else lies the fount of meaning we inflict on our spirit?

In the latest peck of time, some reside under heaven forgotten, and believe the celestial holds no more power over us. Yet, in all temperate regions of the commuting world, there are two vital seasons: that in which the commuter seeks shade, and that in which they seek sun.

Most urban denizens have a varied set of layered fibers with which to combat a multitude of temperatures over the course of a year or a day, from the relentlessly unmoving air of the 23rd Street stop on the R/W train, to the eternally arctic C-Town on Graham and Metropolitan. Even with this necessary adaptive skill learned by all who reside at the mercurial latitudes, not one inhabitant does not mark the moment they turn away from the sun, only to beg its patience four to eight months later. In each of these moments, mortal commuters are reminded that all else is illusion, and everything is permitted beneath the ever-punishing and life-giving god that lights the day.

NEW YORK SWIPE

"No, no, no, that's a *Florida* swipe, man, you have to do the *New York* swipe."

As the Florida swipe is apparently different from the New York swipe to a degree necessitating conversation loud and long enough to be overheard, it is only polite to attempt to explain the New York swipe, so future Floridians might walk through the city's transport access gates without breaking stride.

It would please the mind to assume that anyone navigating swipe-based transportation would know to have their swiping card at hand prior to encountering the gate, but, given the ample evidence, it would be unwise to assume this. This is a shame, as the ability to not break stride while crossing a turnstile is in no small way dependent on the existence of that stride prior to breaching the boundary.

There is an average walking speed that occurs in all public spaces, based on intent, surroundings, and stress. In all New York subway stations, the surroundings are bleak, the stress is high, and the intent is to leave with the minimum necessary human contact, which creates an average walking speed of approximately 2.7 miles, or 4.3 kilometers, per hour. This allows for optimal human avoidance without undue strain on transit time. This speed should decrease by 10 to 20 percent upon reaching the gate, and, if the card is already in the hand at this juncture, the hand motion resupplies that 10 to 20 percent in its forward swiping motion. This hand-body velocity offset provides the delay needed for the swipe to register prior to the midsection hitting the turnstile bar. Some prefer to use this delay to twist a hip forward for bar rotation; others take advantage of the fact that it is exactly enough time to move the swiping hand into position to push the bar ahead of the following midsection. It is the latter who create the convincing illusion that New Yorkers do not slow down when crossing turnstiles, but in both cases, without a preexisting momentum, the offset cannot be instinctively applied, and the swipe speed will likely be misjudged.

Of course, a successful swipe is never guaranteed. Without it, a New Yorker merely grinds their reproductive organs into unyielding metal, and it is well known in the reputable boroughs that such a sensation should only happen if the experience is being purchased from a professional. But happen it does: The age of the card, the caliber of the card reader, and the humidity can turn a frictionless transaction into a fruitless embarrassment.

However, there are certain protocols to minimize the frequency of failed swipes. It is natural to grip the card with the thumb in the middle, depressing the center of the card and creating a concave bend away from the card reader. This natural urge must be overcome. The optimal grip is to hold the card lightly at the top rear, and apply a slight bending pressure away from the body. This gently presses the magnetic strip toward the reader, increasing the odds that this technology will fucking work once in a while.

Thus, with preparation, averaged speed, and optimal grip, any Florida resident can, with minimal practice, execute the New York swipe.

FIELD NOTES: RECOGNITION

If one is blessed with functioning vision, seeing people is an unavoidable consequence of living among them, and the human brain is adept at both practices. Recognizing a human face or figure is one of the more lauded abilities of the brain, trumped only perhaps by its ability to make wild assumptions about the recognized face.

Yet the ability to live among other humans can upstage numerous and supposedly automatic functions of the brain, and I had the pleasure of this experience.

The train was just arriving, and I had to do the slow scan of cars to see if I needed to move to maximize my chances of getting into one. Through the middle of my scan walked the protohuman.

It was mostly matte black, the winter uniform of choice in Manhattan. I think it was female, but I base that judgment solely on the shape of the brownish blob atop what I presumed was the head. The face was absent: a hazy, not-matte-black blob with two fuzzy, colorless blobs where the eyes should have been. There was no other detail. Race, sex, adornment, expression, mood: All were missing. I registered only the overwhelming probability that a human had walked through my field of view. The limited remainder of my attention after a long day was wholly consumed by scanning the train, and I registered more details in the faces behind windows speeding by than I did in the walking human form two feet in front of me. When this limitation combined with a decade of training myself not to ogle strangers or in any way cause discomfort, the cognitive mixture was sufficient to break my facial recognition so completely I noticed it was absent.

To this day, I can recall no significant detail of the protohuman blob. It may have carried a bag. It may have looked directly into my eyes. It may have been smiling. It may have been crying. To me, it remains only the vaguest first strokes of a painter laying the foundation for the shape and shade of a portrait. I still wonder if this is the initial visual experience for seeing all faces, before our mind decides to pay attention and rewrite the fractional second of the past to make us think we're good with faces.

LOCAL TRAFFIC PATTERNS

General skills must always adapt to local conditions. In rural conditions, commuters instinctively understand this, and approach all new roads with attention and awareness (except when they don't, and, at the very least, are quickly removed from that day's commuting population). Urbanites, more absorbed with the movement of people than the lay of the terrain, commonly make two potentially lethal mistakes.

The first is to simply not understand the environment, and assume all intersections are equal. They are not. The change of one streetlight to red does not guarantee the change of its perpendicular companion. Without a countdown, the blinking DON'T WALK signal's duration is an all-but-arbitrary mystery, never to be trusted. Bike lanes are variously busy and even more variously respected by their attendant cyclists. Relative populations of taxis, delivery trucks, and civilian vehicles inform a variable consensus of traffic law, ignored or misread at mortal peril.

The second is to follow the example of the locals before understanding their motives. The person who moves against the light may be aware of a reliable gap in traffic. They may also be suicidal, or extremely drunk. Mere imitation will provide neither speed nor safety in strange lands; the onus is ever upon the stranger to observe, interpret, and adapt.

HITCHHIKING

Though pointlessly difficult in cityscapes, hitchhiking remains a viable, if risky, means of traversing the countryside.

Hitchhiking is first and foremost a lesson in rejection. It is highly recommended to anyone unsympathetic to beggars. It is enlightening to become invisible to the majority of the world's population for taking a particular action due to a pressing need. That said, hitchhiking is a strange sort of activity, oft embarked upon out of desperation to address a spatiotemporal requirement that hitchhiking by its nature is ill-equipped to fulfill. A good rule of thumb is to have enough time to walk to the destination, and hope it doesn't come to that.

Hitchhiking is also a form of commuting for the un- or irregularly employed, and such persons may not be interested in stamping out the temporal uncertainties in their lives. Taken thusly, hitchhiking becomes the purest form of commuting: The commuter no longer makes war with the path when they have mastered themselves, and the commute untethers its end point to flutter freely amid the winds of chance.

STAIRS

The crucible at which the New York commuter lays their dignity upon immovable infrastructure to satisfy irresistible capitalism is the stairway from the L train to the uptown N/Q/R/W.

All stairs are transitional spaces wherein effort is expended in an uneventful progression toward the next place where something may happen. Yet stairs are often bereft of the metaphorical gravity exerted by similar spaces, such as ladders or hills. "Uphill" and "downhill" express negative and positive states of exertion, respectively, as well as negative and positive states of projected fortune, exactly not respectively. "Upstairs" and "downstairs" merely express relative positions on either side of the stairs, allocating nothing to the experience of navigating their common connection. This is an unfortunate failure of imagination: Surely the "glass staircase" could be used to describe the experience of something getting progressively more difficult for no apparent reason and with no obvious destination?

Yet this literary shortcoming exists precisely because stairs tend to be short transitions, neither loved nor dreaded, the most dramatic—and often final—experience of them being falling down a long set.

They do, however, take on a subtly sinister affect in any residential area where the multi-tenant buildings rise above four floors and eschew motorized elevating. It is not a wholly deficient belief system that weighs "sixth-floor walk-up" against "no windows" and finds them equal evils.

(This discounts, of course, those belief systems that do not consider a lack of windows or six floors of stairs evil. However, it can be shown that a preference for one ideologically rejects a preference for the other, so the theoretical belief system that finds both situations appealing can only be itself a particularly radical evil.)

The situation where stairs reveal their true physical and metaphysical power is when they are at once necessary and insufficient.

Departing the L train at Union Square during the morning rush hour is a war won or lost in seconds, for there are only five to spare. The perfectly positioned commuter, near the exit, devoid of obstacle, and sufficiently distant in time from the last train's arrival, can flit up the stairs like a schoolboy from an optimistic BBC special.

Everyone else discovers what it feels like to be a particle of pressurized gas. The stairwell has room for two people abreast, though nearly everyone pretends it can handle three. The diligent souls coming down this stairway in the early hours are an oppressive minority rule, but they are as low on options as the four hundred people funneling themselves into a one-lane stairwell. Offense seems inevitable as some people go to the back of the morass and some try to sneak in the sides, but after those five seconds, all motion becomes prescribed as four hundred boroughers dig through one another for the single passage out of a moldy cavern, a passage wrought small and alone because its makers never expected this many people to choose to trap themselves in debasement.

On the eve of the day, they all come back down, having traveled the dangerously narrow trackside alleys of the

N/Q/R/W platform, and find themselves facing the same funnel as the stairs narrow, and perhaps understand why the people in the morning thought they could keep moving even as the potential span of persons was whittled from four to three to two, but now it's the bastards coming up who refute the possibility of ever being on time for anything.

Postscript

Between writing and publication, the Metropolitan Transportation Authority has greatly improved the state of this particular transfer. The MTA took ninety-eight years to build one-eighth of the 2nd Avenue subway and requires contract negotiations to make coffee; the notion that they could widen a staircase in less time than it takes to edit a short book never crossed the author's mind. However, though this chapter will feel inaccurate to future commuters, it has been left in as a monument to the suffering of prior generations.

FALLING PEBBLE

When the crush of persons outside a train precludes swift motion, one must subsume one's own intentions to the sociophyiscs of the crowd.

The golden practitioner strives to be a falling pebble. As the vessel fills, some or many pebbles may not come to rest in it, but all move closer in the small motions of least resistance. Eventually all pebbles reach a vessel at a shared and steady rate.

All are aware of the damage done by a tumbling boulder in this situation. However, it is equally important not to be a stuck stone, forcing constricted flows of pebbles around it. In all cases, strive to be as one with the natural flow of the environment.

LAYERING

Temperature changes over a commute can be severe, particularly if it involves one or more transportation systems. They are also unpredictable: A crowded train is hotter than an empty one, to say nothing of broken temperature-control systems. Even beyond the commute, the confines of the office produce daily dispute over the numbers on the thermostat, as a hundred or more disparate constitutions, weakened by years of office work, attempt to cope with a shared environment.

A large jacket of great warmth may seem the most efficient way to stave off cold, but it is simply untenable in this situation. When dependent on public transport in colder climates, it is necessary to master the art of layering.

Though every commuter finds their own methodology, the following is a common template.

First, a wicking layer. A kind of thin, form-fitting garment that copes with moisture and defends the skin from errant breezes penetrating the outer layers. These can be surprisingly warm, so should only be used during the coldest months.

Next is a securing layer. A shirt or dress to keep the wicking layer close to the skin. This is also referred to as the presentation layer, as it is what people will see for most of the day, unless employed by that special kind of soul who thinks a few dollars is sufficient compensation for the persistent suffering of dozens. Since those souls are not at all special in the sense of being rare, the next layer is called the mediation layer: a thin sweater, sweatshirt, or hoodie, largely used to manage office fluctuations.

Near the top, a sports layer. The relationship between the sports layer and the mediation layer is where the most negotiation happens to modulate warmth and bulk. One can be discarded on warmer days, and it helps to have a variety of each with varying thickness and insulation. Whatever the combination, it is highly recommended that the sports layer have a working zipper for quick adaptation to small climate shifts.

At this point, particularly with natural winter accoutrements such as scarves and hats, the commuter is already fairly warm and prepared. To top it off, they should have at least two coats. The first should be a light to medium coat to serve as windbreaker and scarf-securer. The other should be a large jacket of great warmth, because sometimes it's just too goddamn cold.

FIELD NOTES: EXCUSE ME

Subject A boarded an uptown 5 train in New York City. The train was well past the tipping point. Subject A, pushed from behind deeper into the occupants, caught briefly on a purse hanging off subject B. Subject B proceeded to angrily yank the purse back to its initial position and shout, "Excuse me is a word!"

Observations: Subject B was incorrect. "Excuse me" is a phrase.

BICYCLES

In any city dominated by a chaotic mixing of public and private transportation, bicycles are a not-repentant-enough scourge on the patience of better people.

An individual bicyclist may not be the worst human in a given metropolis, but they are likely not a paragon of consideration, and given the lack of said paragons to counter the scourge, an individual bicyclist likely contributes to the problem.

It is true that a deliverer of goods riding the two-wheeled mechanical engine at the crosswalk has reasons for their behavior. Surely, this one-way road can be flexible in its monodirectional demand when the target of my package is halfway down the block, and the legal recourse is three avenues of danger. Yet the first sin is never the last. The human conscience, faced with growing burdens, shows ever greater agility in shrugging off ever greater offenses to its purpose. When finally faced with the unconscionable and irredeemable weight of a thousand lights ignored, pedestrians clipped, cars cut off, and all variants of signs ignored, the conscience implodes, ceding its necessary function to the stronger urge of indignation, and all its failures become the failures of others, its own cruelties projected onto the blurred faces of innocents sweeping past at 20 to 30 miles per hour. There's little need to ponder the terrors enacted by amateur cyclists when the professionals have wrought such horror on the human condition.

And yet. The horseless carriage is still a greater threat to our future than the horseless horse. The word "bicycle" has never been popularly associated with the phrase "millions dead," and whatever pains are necessary to remove that phrase from our vocabulary are arguably worthwhile. But considering the pursuit worthwhile is not the same as forgiving the manner in which it is pursued, and the inevitable narcissism of the urban bicyclist is the only explanation for the following two incidents:

First, a bicycle chained to a subway pole at rush hour.

Feel the words in your mouth. The cyclist who takes their bicycle on the subway is already lacking in shame and subject to scorn, but they have either their reasons or their pride, and at least cop to the offense. Whosoever chains their bike to the pole demonstrates total disregard for both personal and social responsibility, and in the same action marks themselves a coward to a degree unmatched in all of literature.

Second, a man, on a phone, holding his bike perpendicular to the flow of traffic in the middle of a sidewalk at six in the afternoon.

The mentality of a person who commits this act is unknowable. Perhaps they desire violence. Perhaps the ire of strangers excites them, or lifts a loneliness they can neither escape nor abide. Whatever they tell themselves and whatever their therapists make note of, it is obvious their parents did not waste love on their upbringing. The diminutive measure of such a person's soul defies calculation, but the bicycle enables the expression of their empty spirit.

From the approximate geographic center of the greater metropolitan New York area, it takes just under two hours to exit the city in any meaningful sense. Technically, it is possible to reach New Jersey in less than this time, but, again technically, the riverside part of New Jersey is a green-card borough to which we refuse citizenship.

One need not live at the very heart of the beast for this phenomenon to phenom; one needs only to be sufficiently buried in the mangled tissue between borders and airports and trains that spend enough time aboveground to get base tans. [Editor's note: The PATH train does in fact look like it has a tan, but it's spray-on.] From these interstitial depths, there is simply no sufficient combination of motorized transit that can achieve escape velocity in less than 108 minutes.

Some residents, clinging to some flickering illusion of freedom, maintain cars, against all probability of parking. There are hidden pathways known to the elder cabbies that break relative space across vast tracts of the inner city, but even these cannot efficiently circumvent the great arteries that connect the city's traffic to more civilized roads. If the intent is to exit the city with intact autonomy, plan the trip to begin at 4:30 a.m., after the last drunk has crashed but before the industrial deliveries get in full swing.

If the MTA chicken-bone readers have received good news, the subways will provide passage to a major train line or an airport, as long as this airport is not LaGuardia, in which case the MTA will not provide means of getting there and the airplane probably won't leave even if the cab gets there in time. JFK and Newark will at least eventually emit a plane, and a very lucky series of events will get a commuter from their door to noncity airspace in a reasonable time frame.

Quasi-natives who use some of the larger semicommuting, city-exiting trains will often confuse non-natives by saying it takes them "about an hour" to get from their Connecticut home to their place of work. This confusion arises because a standard New York hour is what most people refer to as "seventy-five minutes," and that described hour in fact only includes the passage from Connecticut to Grand Central, and not the ensuing subway or pedestrian journeys. This is a forgivable misunderstanding, because another little-known fact about New York is that, once a person is in the city and has two bars of cell phone reception, they are at work. This is true even if they are sleeping, visiting, or unemployed, the only escapes being 108-minute journeys and death.

CHANGE

A commute by its nature creates routine, a steady and predictable path through an uncertain universe. It is a cultivated rut, full of knowns and known unknowns, predictable alterations, familiar coffee shops, landmarks that don't so much mark the land as they lull the mind into meditative travel. A car taken down a road driven a thousand times is automatically gassed and braked by trained feet sensitive to the most fleeting images from the eyes and the most subtle variations in the road. A sidewalk is similarly navigated by a flowing gestalt of recognition, the mind's only concern the trajectory of other bodies in relation to its own.

Perhaps this is a failing. The comfort of engaging existential automata degrades ontological engagement, allowing the mind to occupy itself less with knowing itself and its environment, and more with the anxiety of frustrated desires. Yet there is also comfort in the much-maligned rut. A rut signals the possibility that tomorrow will be the same, which—for better or worse—allows the greater fears to be put off an hour, a day, or a year. It provides the illusion of stability, and that illusion is the bedrock upon which all of civilization is built, and even if it is built on the backs of we the delusional, we crave its comfort. Even our most outlandish fantasies are only of our own better tomorrows; the better world those tomorrows might contain is a side effect.

A change in routine sends the mind back to its last change in routine. We are composed of many threads, and each thread is as old as the last time it was knotted to a new companion. A change in commute upsets these threads in unpredictable ways with unpredictable severity. If an office moves, the people and the job are the same, but the path is altered. Perhaps the job changes, but the path is nearly the same. If the new path is too close to the old, it's both surprising and unsurprising to arrive at the former office. New coffee shops must be discovered, coffee shops that may have never heard of your order.

Re-engagement with the environment is necessary. In a city, exiting public transportation reminds the commuter of the arbitrary attribution of compass points to a tangle of roads; in a suburb, the endless repetition must be recracked for the subtle differentiation that might mark a point of navigation; in the country, whole new lands must be learned and paths forged across a dearth of choice. A thread of the self is unbound and knotted to a new tapestry of space and people. A new and necessary path is writ upon the internal map of the world, even as the old path rejects total erasure, and the mind becomes more complex as it navigates a new slice of the world, and, inevitably, erodes its claim to autonomous individuality. For how can a mind cling to hubris when it is so flummoxed and utterly absorbed in simply trying to walk the right way down a new street? A change in commute puts us at our most nakedly human, for even the most pious commuter knows no god that would intercede. All navigate the new alone.

ON THE ISSUE OF MUGGING

In any metropolis, ambulation involves an inherent risk of pedestrian robbery, or "mugging," as it is commonly known in English. There is no absolute rational course of action to counter an irrational act, so take the following as a means of maximizing the probability of an unimpeded journey, and certainly not as a salve to all the ills of a broken culture.

When walking in familiar or unfamiliar urban environments, it is best to appear angry, native, poor, and unarmed.

Each of these adjectives invites debate, but let us examine them through the harsh lens of trying to get somewhere for the sake of a paycheck. This lens provides an unambiguous clarity.

Anger and nativity tend to dovetail in complex urban environments, for reasons outlined in many other chapters of this book. The stubborn difficulty of well-known and well-worn paths fans a constant flame of anger as the commuter wonders why this isn't getting any easier after all these years. That anger is the mark of a native, so any potential mugger must consider the target one who will be here again and who may no longer consider death an unacceptable alternative to the rest of their journey.

Dissuading a potential mugger is no more simply achieved than by appearing poor. One need not look destitute, but a certain scruff about the face and wear in the coat will at least make one look unworthy of the effort.

Finally, appearing unarmed will reduce the risk of a potential mugger making a preemptive move toward incapacitation. Once selected as a target, it is best to appear an easy one in order to maximize the odds of a smooth and injury-free business transaction. The ideal outcome is to be able to have a good story to tell friends. This is infinitely preferable to asking nurses confused questions upon waking up.

Of course, all of this merely reduces the odds, as it relies on a modicum of rational action from hypothetical muggers. Since mugging is rarely a rational action to begin with, keep the head down and the cash handy, and be prepared to pay one of the many unfair tolls on the highway of life.

EVERY CONVERSATION ABOUT PUBLIC TRANSIT IN NEW YORK CITY

"Oh, man, the trains. That line was a mess. Just a complete mess."

"Oi, you took that line? I was just going to complain about this line."

"Oh, this line is terrible. That line is pretty good most of the time, but tonight . . ."

"Sick passenger?"

"Train traffic."

"Always a lie."

"Always."

"You know, it's not the lie, it's the wait."

"Oh, of course. You know they're lying—"

"But they won't tell you when."

"And they won't tell you they don't know when."

"Because you'll leave."

"Because we'll leave."

"Fucking unions."

"Fucking government."

"Fucking people!"

"I know, right?"

"There was this idiot on the platform this morning . . ."

"Oh, God, the idiots."

"I know, right?"

"I had one yesterday."

"Impeded your movement, did he?"

"God, how didn't he?"

"Assholes."

"Fucking people."

"Fucking trains."

"Fucking buses."
"Cheaper than a car, though."
"Oh, Christ, the parking alone."
"Those poor bastards."

FIELD NOTES: GROUNDHOG COMMUTING

Wherever a new job lies, the habitual commute emerges quickly and is fairly immutable. There is nearly always a fastest route, and barring construction, dead trains, or desperation for variety, there's no reason to change it. Given two or more paths nearly equal in length, I switch between them, but even that switching will start to take on a predictable pattern.

When walking through Manhattan, the regularity of the experience can be shocking. Previously, when leaving from my girlfriend's apartment, I would get my coffee, walk down to Grand, turn right, cross Forsyth, turn left at Chrystie and walk next to the park, then right at Hester, after which it was a straight shot to Baxter.

Unfortunately, I always ended up having to wait for a light when crossing Chrystie at Hester, which meant always having to wait for a light at Bowery, and those are both long, cold lights during much of the year. This bothered me, as it violated the principle of continual motion. I eventually noticed that every time I got to Chrystie, the light was about to change in my favor, so I decided to risk the nasty stretch of Grand between Chrystie and Bowery in the hopes that it would get me to Bowery in time. Unfortunately, the stretch is bad enough that it's always about five seconds too slow to make the very short light on the other side.

Still, that put me in the game on the long block of Bowery between Grand and Hester. This block is pretty clear, except for one guy handing out restaurant flyers approximately thirty feet south of the Grand and Bowery corner, and I walk pretty fast, but there isn't quite enough time to make it the whole length of the block before the lights cycle back to the long wait. However, since traffic is pretty clear, when the light turns, I can cross about thirty-five feet before the actual crosswalk and weave through the stopped cars on the far side, thus traversing the Chrystie/Bowery portion without stopping.

To summarize: wait five to ten seconds at Grand and Chrystie. Forty seconds down Grand, turn left, pass the flyer guy at thirty feet on the right, cross thirty-five feet before the crosswalk.

Every. Single. Time.

And it will be exactly like that until someone changes the timing on the lights or the weather warms up and slows everybody down. Though today a guy crossed the sidewalk in front of me with a freshly butchered pig over his shoulder, so that was new.

DECISIONS

The snaggle of paths in and around the New York subway ask difficult questions of travelers when one of the paths inevitably ceases to function. Await the repair and eventual train, sometimes twenty minutes away, sometimes an hour, sometimes a day? Walk three avenues to take a different train to another hub? If the destination is a ten-minute walk, is it worthwhile to wait for the local connection? Each minute spent waiting is a minute delayed, but the grates above the subway lines impart a terrible knowledge: Once deciding to walk, the commuter will know upon exiting a station if the long-awaited train has just arrived, and their decision only lengthened the journey by eight minutes.

When the rivers become uncrossable, the chasm between past expectation and future necessity belies the very notion of self-determination. At the end of the day, simply eating dinner or getting a drink on the wrong side of the river becomes as rational as any other course of action; the path must eventually clear itself, and two hours here are as good as two hours in any other warren of the boroughs, and even if a taxi is an economically viable option, they are all busy and twice as expensive. In the mornings, the lucky give up and go home; the rest rush to subway maps and trace unfamiliar paths with hungry eyes, praying the number of minutes they quote on their apologetic phone call bears vague resemblance to the new reality they will endure upon finding a possible route.

At peak hours, the decision is between finding a position on a car optimal for disembarking and a position on a car that can actually be boarded. These cars are never, ever the same, unless the stop in question is in an affordable neighborhood.

Sometimes the decision is whether to do something.

Every single day, there will be a fight. Every single day, there will be a homeless person or ten. Every single day, there will be something that inspires discomfort, inflicts anger, or invites sadness. When these moments happen, there is probably not enough time to reason out a response that will satisfy the Moral History of You, but there will soon be enough time to rationalize the response given two minutes ago while marching down a stairwell or dodging a family of five that didn't know where they're going or, worse, didn't care when they got there.

The fight will happen on the far side of the train, and the ear will only hear the expletives, each one grabbing your attention, but not quite enough of it to suss out the details, only enough to locate the source of the "fucking bitch" or the "you gonna do something about it?" that alert and re-alert the survival instinct.

The homeless person will register on a multivariate system measuring age, aggressiveness, skin color, readability of signage, position in traffic flow, and a rough estimate of how savagely they were betrayed by the fine print of the social contract. They will almost always be found wanting.

The greater the concentration of people, the greater the binding force of social momentum. Ego buckles under the weight of indifference, and most reach for the prosthesis of passive decency. Yet the weight is borne, not discarded, and some egos will not suffer the blind eye, and they will disturb the balances of all who struggle to live quietly. And then a choice is bleakly presented: Must I act? Am I preventing something, or making something worse? If a mother is threatening to beat her child on a crowded platform, is there anything I can do? Anything I should do? Will I ever know the answer, whether I act or not?

PHASE

Pedestrian pathways undergo identifiable phase transitions as the density of traffic increases, each informing the traffic's constituent groups' and individuals' ideal tactical motion.

Empty or nearly empty pathways provide little hindrance to the activity of a group. Personal space is the business of the individual and their immediate relationships. Indeed, it is often seen as rude to infringe on any stranger's sense beyond necessary sight; even sound and smell are expected to be kept to a minimum when there is the possibility of doing so. Further constraints are personal or cultural.

Once there is enough foot to call traffic, a notional order is called for. Though there are usually no official directional lanes, following the temporary flows is expected. In all but the widest paved throughways, the outside maximal width of a group is two abreast, and most seasoned commuters will naturally adopt this pattern. Awareness of others becomes—or should become—constant instead of intermittent.

The next shift occurs when any prohibition against bodily contact becomes untenable. There is simply not enough room. The path can still be navigated by individuals; groups cannot be kept together in any social sense without a maximum of unpleasantness. Groups of two tether by sight in single file; any larger group must rely on its component individuals' navigational skills to reconvene in sparser contexts. Identity subsumes to communal flow:

All instincts are brought into play in frame-by-frame path-finding. There is no time.

The final phase is the state in which constant physical contact is mandatory. This transition rarely occurs outside transportation vessels or excessively popular musical acts. All motion is forced; the very notion of identity becomes ill-defined, even as the ego rages in isolation. To move alone is to battle entropy itself. Here is human condition reduced to space and need, as desire crumbles between the force of flesh and the prison of the body.

TAXI

Since no potentially transportive artery of a busy metropolis goes unclogged during rush hours, the bourgeois expense of personal livery is no guarantee of speed or efficacy in a commute. Indeed, road congestion is the manifestation of thousands of frustrated wills, more dangerous and unpredictable by far than a simple trash fire in a subway tunnel. No, a taxi is desperate resort, when the trash fires win and there is no other means short of a long and windy walk.

The taxi driver is a curious player in this: For them it could be said the entire workday is commuting. They are the white blood cells in the city's constant war to move people between the gears of capitalism a little faster. Ever rushing with the breath of the city, they map its tracts of consumption as the rails and buses map its means of production.

This makes them extremely dangerous. To a taxi driver, the principles of commuting are not abstractions applied to twice-daily routine; they are the skills tied directly to income. Taxi drivers are the true masters of the commute, residing on peaks incomprehensible to civilian workers. The danger comes—as it so often does—when mastery is accompanied by its wretched parasite, hubris. Hubris is the enemy of awareness, and those who drive without awareness, no matter their skill, drive a single lane toward catastrophe.

STREET CROSSING

There are three approaches to waiting for a walk signal. Locals and tourists alike often opt for the least advisable option: watching the people. People like to follow people. Everyone knows it, everyone does it, and it never becomes a better idea. Midtown streets answer the question, "If all your friends walked off a cliff, would you?" and the answer is a long and fading scream followed by a thud. People who want to be liked generally watch the people, as do people too preoccupied to take the next most common option: watching the lights.

Rule-oriented people start with watching the lights, and these people are generally the most surprised and offended when they're hurled into the air by the cars driven by people not watching anything. People not watching anything are often driving cars in the city, so if someone lives through their first year of commuting, it's because they took the survival-oriented option: watching the cars. People have a death wish and traffic lights are merely strong suggestions, but if there are no cars moving toward you, you can almost guarantee you won't get hit by one.

The very best strategy is to use all three options, in order of importance. First, check the cars. Once they stop moving, check the light. Not because it matters that much what the light says, but because it provides a baseline for managing expectations. Finally, watch the people, because once the cars are absent or stationary, people are the primary adversaries. At this stage, remember that when taking cues from others, note the cautious, because if they know something you don't, they could save your life, and ignore the eager, because if they don't know something you should, they might get you killed.

FIELD NOTES: KNOCK YO' ASS OUT

The management of aggression, both one's own and that of one's fellow commuters, becomes crucial in the many choke points encountered near turnstiles. Once past the turnstile, a predatory instinct takes over, given that the choke points are the difference between a thirty-second exit and a five-minute trudge resembling honey exiting a funnel. It was at one of these points that a hurrying and harried man of minor stature decided to navigate via elbow and excuse-mes through the mortal morass.

The logical balance between personal ire and the prodding of the oblivious—or simply stupid—is of course passive-aggressive exhalations and barely audible utterances theorizing on the species of the offending commuter's sexual partners. In this instance, I failed to rein in my instincts, and gently, but firmly, moved my elbow back into place after it was pushed aside. This elicited the "Aw, no, son" that I intuited marked the beginning of a rapid decline in the quality of my evening.

I regretted my slip at once.

"Yo, I will knock yo' ass out. I had a hard day, punk." Could he not entertain the possibility that my workday contained its own difficulties? That my own personality, the thin veil of social reflexes hiding my jungle lusts, was also fraying, ready to blow away before the gust of a breath spent in anger?

He could not. I fear the body of data that could convey the subtlety of another's motivation would find insufficient space to unfold in his means of contemplation. I was left with a choice: de-escalate, or embrace the long-awaited moment of being driven too far.

Facing down one's own anger is a tricky dance. Anger flows freely, and lacks a well-defined channel: Direct it inward and it will only build pressure, awaiting a leak; direct it outward and the body seeks to maintain the explosion. With physical violence on the line, fear compounds the anger: The fear of pain, the fear of one's own anger undoing a lifetime's worth of civil practice, the fear of the anger being fed by fear feeding the anger, a self-sustaining spiral of rage and pain wanting nothing more than to drop the mask and go screaming into battle.

"Oh, for fuck's sake," I muttered, keeping my eyes forward as I tried to hang on to the drowning memory of all the things I had left to lose, choice among them a promising date with an attractive dancer on the far side of the tunnel between 5th and 6th avenues. My antagonist started doing the inebriated shuffle that signals both the desire to fight and the complete inability to do so. I tried to breathe.

"You want this, motherfucker? I will fuck you up, just test me."

Breathe in. Calm. Breathe out. You should be left a beaten husk in the middle of the tunnel, broken nose bleeding on the ground, with my shoe on your neck and my elbow working its way through your ocular socket while I sweetly whisper in your ear, "How's your day going now, dickwad?"

Instead I said, "That was aggressive, I apologize." I made a point of demonstrating that my speech was more eloquent, and my voice louder, stronger, and harder than his, and declined to dignify him with a glance. He dropped his "guard" and shuffled away, unsure of whether he won. He muttered several inaudible phrases as he increased his distance from me, and kept glancing back. He dimly knew he lost the fight he wanted to win with his threat, because it was clear I was not afraid, but he lacked the wit to continue the verbal conflict after an explicit apology. But he won the fight I fought, because he was a bully I won't soon forget, and he made me doubt my commitment to decency. Perhaps he should be trained out of violence with violence. I've never seen the practice succeed, and I don't believe it can ever create more than slavery, resentment, and revolt. But he made me question my convictions, albeit briefly, by threatening my body, and tempting me into satisfying my own weaknesses.

But I did not. I let him go. I walked a few blocks to clear my head, and had dinner with my date. That evening, I ejaculated upon her breasts. It was glorious.

DODGING

People take cues from other people's eyes to determine which way they're going to veer to circumvent a given human obstacle. Hence there is more awkward shuffling as people second-guess each other's path in the summer, because everyone's wearing shades and nobody can tell where anyone else is looking.

The mechanics are straightforward: Two people are looking where they are going. They are primarily scanning for openings and calculating the velocities of people converging on the openings. When a collision is imminent, person A scans the head of person B to see where it is scanning. B is generally scanning over one shoulder or the other of A, so A goes in the opposite direction to the best of their ability. This process short-circuits if A and B scan each other at the same time, because they'll both be waiting for a cue. As they get closer, a sharp turn of the head will signal the other, and they'll diverge. Sometimes this need to be a full body gesture, and sometimes a Hail Mary dodge is necessary. If all this fails, or competing Hail Marys collide, both parties are reduced to the stop-and-shuffle.

An experienced commuter will note the basic fallacy of this theory: Most people aren't watching where they are going. However, in heavily officed areas mostly free of distraction and full of local workers, the theory is sound. There are subtle but noticeable tilts of the head indicating on which side the oncoming traffic means to pass, and even after checking for traffic at crossings, the head comes back to indicate its intended path. Following the head is at least a functional tactic, if not reliable enough to be called a principle.

CANVASSERS

"No! Get in the way! Be unavoidable!" This shout by one canvasser to another, who had just politely stepped out of the way, illustrates the heart of the dilemma.

Canvassers are antithetical to the core principles of commuting. The commuter is trying above all else to ignore and keep moving; the canvasser is doing everything they can to get people to stop and pay attention.

There is valid sympathy to be had for the unending river of rejection a canvasser endures, but not nearly enough to stop. No matter how righteous their cause, they are invariably asking the commuter to slow down and spend money at the exact moment they have to hurry up to make money. Ironically, were they to canvass in any place where people congregated for aimless and unhurried recreation, they would be asked to leave. They are forced to operate where nearly all traffic is commuting.

Part of the problem is that canvassing technology seems stuck in the 1980s. Even if not hurrying, even if the cause weighs heavily on the passerby, they are likely to keep passing by before they fill out a credit card form by hand. There are people getting credit cards today who don't even know this is possible, and it would do the canvasser and softhearted commuter alike a great service to equip the canvasser with an Apple Pay reader.

Public transport entails a period of helplessness with limited options for filling the time.

Reading remains a mainstay, its domain little encroached upon by the portable media of modernity. But encroach it does, and games and television are as common as words from any medium.

For some, what I assume is music is sufficient for their mental detachment. Others have no option but to maintain control over children, their own or on loan, and that creates a reality entirely separate from the trivial doldrums of commuting.

All in their way find some escape for the locus of their attention, and they become quite good at it. Naturally, a certain kind of temperament takes personal offense at the habits of others, and derides this form of escape. Such persons encourage haranguing trapped strangers under the guise of "human connection" or some other rubbish. Less ghastly are those who encourage meditation.

Both kinds of malcontents fail to see the irony of their arguments because they cannot recognize their own retreats from or into themselves as escapes. There is a romantic notion that there is a perfect form of engaging with the world that will elevate a mortal life above a series of brief distractions along a tedious journey dictated by faceless forces. The master commuter recognizes life as dust, and procures the least taxing means of avoiding that truth.

All escapes are little oblivions: temporary freedoms from the flesh-bound self and its hungers. With them comes the power of familiarity, a brace for the necessary courage to walk among the great oblivions that surround and define human existence in space and time.

FIELD NOTES: PERSISTENCE

The kid directly in front of me in the turnstile line is already in rough shape. For some reason, this entrance to the Canal Street station is always less a line of people than a confused amoeba trying to navigate through a sieve. Even hardened commuters' eyes get twitchy here. The kid looks like he's trying to stay above it all, the way teenagers do, by looking mopey and sullen. I believe he's stoned. In thirty seconds I will be sure of it.

It's one of those moments when you just can't believe you share a species with some of its members. The kid has a skateboard strapped horizontally across his backpack. Due to his slouching, he's stopped by the waist high portion of the turnstile after he slides his card through the reader. He simply straightens his body, and, perhaps believing that the apparent similarity of width between the lower and upper portions of the entry is merely an optical illusion, walks forward and is again stopped when his skateboard hits the sides. He looks confused. I move on through an sudden opening on my left, wishing it was less crowded so I could see the fallout.

Few things in life are as disheartening as watching a grown human fail to understand object persistence. When I left, he was backing out and into the angry amoeba behind him. For the sake of us all, I hope he turned sideways, but I can picture him trying another turnstile.

DIGITIZED

In the early information age, any work that involved processing information found itself less in need of a place of work. New forms of work evolved from this ever-increasing flow of data. Slowly at first, with text going hyper, then exponentially faster as the tubes widened and data was fractally compressed, until the only sets of working data that couldn't be flung over a cheap router were those that only existed in and because of the massive connective infrastructure.

Klick for click, the vast majority of commuting is now done across wires and radio waves, if not literally bouncing through space between satellite and dish. One might have—and indeed many did—assume this would ease the burdens of the industrial revolution, and release at least white-collar workers from the necessary burden of the commute.

It did not. Technology built in the rarified confines of superconductor laboratories and rural basements tacked itself on to the telestructure and changed the world by force, burrowing through the natural fear of change with power so obvious it couldn't be understood.

Until it was. The gatekeepers of the socioeconomic homogeneity did not claim their keys by accident. They may not have understood the details of the paradigm shift before them, but they understood that the currency of information had metastasized, conveniently within a culture of arrogance and obsession all but begging to be exploited. And to exploit a thing requires the thing to be under a watchful eye, particularly when said thing is versed in navigating the infinite sea of possibility they helped build.

So on they commute to drab and crowded rooms, their burdens doubled and tripled, worked to capacity until they have none. All this is done knowing it need not be, but is, and always will be. The dream of electric abstraction will never be granted to its builders until its controllers have no use for it, or them.

STREETWALKERS

For all the pain caused by those who court death, it is a mere pebble in the gravel pit of agony caused by those who seem unaware of it.

No road in any landscape is free of them. Relying on the general population's aversion to random homicide, they stride through intersections, stroll along highways, and stand in the middle of the street, apparently oblivious to the thousands of tons of speeding metal piloted by humans with smartphones.

They stop traffic and ignore horns, wholly consumed by their apparently irresistible desire to acquire whatever they want immediately, yet they never hurry. To them, the world presents itself as their own backyard, full of intrusive strangers they magnanimously indulge.

This is not far from the solipsistic core in all of us, whispering the debasement of all with whom we share the world. Streetwalkers turn these whispers into passive yet brazen aggression, perhaps even hoping for a challenge that will lead to active aggression.

As with all attention addicts, the only recourses are ignore or execute. Whatever your choice: Godspeed.

EYE CONTACT

The purported meeting of souls that occurs when irises align is immensely overstated. What does take place is the mutual signaling of attention, followed by interpretation of intention.

Even for the master commuter, this is a problem.

The recognition of attention entwines the destinies of all four eyes. (This instant connection does not happen with one-eyed persons, because their two-eyed counterpart cannot quickly ascertain what the monocular traveler is looking at.) Once entwined, the owner of each set makes reflexive assumptions about the intentions behind the other set. These assumptions can be summarily discounted as incorrect; the exceptions are so rare that they vanish in any respectable margin of error.

This puts the two commuters in an immediate state of miscommunication. If they are of similar and untemperamental temperament, they may continue with verbal or nonverbal communication, or simply glance away, keeping their conclusions to themselves, forgotten as quickly as an unmentioned dream. Sadly, accusation and violence are the hallmarks of miscommunication.

The golden practitioner seeks to minimize eye contact, and, when it cannot be avoided, resist the temptation to create the other's personality and motivation for them. Such practitioners understand that the looks shared between those long known to each other carry significance because the lookers have thoroughly built and tested models of both their roles in the relationship. The looks between strangers are simple accidents of applied navigation, and need not bear the burden of misbegotten diplomacy.

CARTOGRAPHY

In the beginning, the wanderers drew maps. For thousands of years, the next travelers bought maps. Then there was GPS, but it wasn't very good, so people still bought maps. Then there was Google Maps, and people printed little maps right before dates and job interviews. Then came the iPhone, and now people just buy iPhones.

In all its forms, the map is used for the first journey. The human mind is a mind of spatial memory, and a path trod once is trod again with far greater ease than remembering even why it's being trod. A large collection of maps once evidenced many journeys; now everyone has an effectively complete map even if they've never left their living room.

Whether measured in paper or bandwidth, the variety of a life can be measured by its need of maps. The mere use of maps can mean many things. Eyes lingering on a lonely island or a distant fjord may not be remembering, but desiring, projecting a feeling to a place and wishing to stand at its edge. The motivation behind the gaze may be as simple as seeking a break from a monotonous and mapless daily journey. It may be something primal: to find a blurry corner of this near-perfect map and squint, perchance to draw.

FIELD NOTES: UP THE DOWN SIDE

I was descending the stairs to the F train at 34th Street. Two trains had pulled into the station, providing an intimidating mass of people to ascend the stairs I was attempting to descend. I didn't expect trouble in this, since it was a two-lane stairway, of the sort where two can walk abreast on either side of the dividing handrail. I followed the recommended procedure when navigating such a stairway during a two-train exodus, which is to slither down the right-hand wall and sigh loudly at the people looking at their feet on their way up.

Then I saw her.

At first, I thought she had dropped something, and had turned around to pick it up and apologize to the man behind her. She was on the left side of the right lane, and was holding things in both hands, so was clearly physically capable of descending stairs without the aid of the center rail. She made a slightly huffy shrug, and I expected her to turn around after her forthcoming apology.

Then I heard her.

Few words have ever caused me as much pain as the five whining syllables that exited her speaking orifice in the next one-point-two seconds.

"This is the down side."

Uttered as if the fourteen angry people stopped in front of her were mentally handicapped for not shuffling into an orderly line on the other side of the stairway, so she, I, and the dozen or so others going down could have our preferred space while the hundreds exiting the train added a few more minutes to their journey.

If I were a quicker, stronger man, I would have grabbed her by the shoulders and forced her to slither down the wall with the rest of us. Alas, I am not, and I tried to make my way past without incident. The man directly in front of the whining madwoman just looked straight through her, as if defeated, escaping to the quieter caves of his mind until she gave up, or was attacked by someone else. The woman behind him was more proactive: She screamed, "Are you fucking kidding me, you idiot bitch?" and dived around them, directly into me. Being of the thinner persuasion, I was able to navigate this extra spatial intrusion and make it off the stairway.

I heard the ensuing argument halfway across the station. Madness is an opponent no tactic can fight but for opportunity and shame.

FERRY

Of all the nonautonomous modes of commuting, the ferry is the most contemplative. Perhaps it is the perceived vulnerability while floating above unknown depths. Perhaps it is the nausea.

With only slightly more mastery over one's fate than when flying, the ferry ride leaves the mind to itself as it makes the most storied transition: the crossing of water. Water is the great known unknown, deep with dangers that usually leave you alone, and an entire world of life living in dimensions that dwarf our thin layer of earthy biology. The surface breached by bows is an intemperate plane between kingdoms, forever separated no matter the diplomacy of their dignitaries.

Our dominion over the land owes much to our navigating this border. Our poetic notions of freedom oft pull metaphor from wave and sail. Yet the true ocean world forbids us its freedoms, freedoms that mock Magellan's pipiest dreams. For all that, its inhabitants' commutes seem as crowded, lonely, and dangerous as ours, and sometimes thousands of miles long. Life finds a way, then wanders back and forth along the way until it dies.

You can also usually find a seat on a ferry.

RESOURCE CONSUMPTION

The resources of a commuter are space, time, and patience, and they maintain complex relationships. Although a reasonable initial allotment of time will grant a proportional abundance of patience, excessive consumption of time drains patience exponentially, as the experience of losing time imposes a greater strain than not having any in the first place. When time is already short, patience is commensurate with its brevity, but with helplessness (and it is indeed a helpless predicament, as time cannot be regained) comes resignation, which assigns a lower limit to patience.

Space has a straightforwardly inverse relationship with patience, with the rate of patience loss in limited space increasing dramatically over time, regardless of how much time a commuter has to work with.

It is broadly believed that patience is the most mutable of these resources, but this is a fallacy predicated on individual exceptionalism, which has no place in a commute shared by many. Commuting among others is a process of negotiation, and space is the most negotiable resource. Effective space negotiations can increase patience reserves and—as Einstein demonstrated—even reduce overall time consumption.

The golden practitioner will embark with strong reserves of time and patience, and aspire to optimal space negotiation.

JAPAN

To a Western commuter, the question might seem absurd: Is it possible for a public transportation system to care about you?

And yet.

The swiftness with which the trains sweep across the island of Japan is the very least of their surprises, though it is indeed surprising to travel eleven hundred kilometers in two days without being especially put out or even losing much of the days to that travel.

Equally unsurprising is the strict yet friendly professionalism on display at all times from staff and passengers alike. This is, after all, what Japan is famous for, after the bizarre sexual media that rubbed out from the cultural friction during the postwar occupation.

Edging toward surprising is the fact that every public transport station looks like it opened yesterday. Though no one would eat off the floors by choice, there is reason to believe no one would suffer unduly if circumstances demanded it.

Outright stunning is the ample legroom, which becomes even more surprising for a tall person in a short country.

But the thing that ties it all together is that each seat has on its back a map of the train car and its nearest neighbors. An elegant achievement in design, it depicts all exits, bathrooms, storage bays, and the occasional smoking closet with clear images and a smatter of text. Every map is relative to its car. It smacks of effort, and once seen, it illuminates the fact that the same effort went into every aspect of the transportation system. Buying tickets for the Kyoto subway is easy after a brief introduction to the system, while many native New Yorkers still seem to have issues adding five dollars to their MetroCards. Labyrinthine train stations connecting several different kinds of transport are easily navigated by clear signs, while many risk starvation in their attempts to exit Penn Station. Every step of travel in Japan seems coordinated and tailored, with precision, to the needs of every traveler in every location.

It may dally with a foolish poetry to consider the possibility that a collection of plastic, steel, electricity, and middle-income employees cares about its commuters in a manner as personal as it feels.

However, it is less of a of stretch to propose an active hostility emanating from the transportation in certain other countries.

PRE-COMMUTING

It is not hard for the average office worker to forget that their morning tends to begin after much of the workforce has already taken its first break. The crush of the nine-to-five office workers that comprises rush hour comes after the slower, more staggered commutes of the people who maintain the infrastructure and provide the services that support the businesses full of people who shuffle data and imaginary money.

The city that never sleeps stirs groggily from its half-conscious daydreaming at around five in the morning, downs its coffee, and is hard at work by eight thirty. The morning begun at the hour of rush is an invasion of already bustling commercial space that most assume magically appears at eight forty-five.

Commuting at seven to a nine-to-five job is a serene experience. Because the noise hasn't hit its stride, the engines revving and gates screeching are starker for the quiet. Because the sidewalk population is still far below critical density, commuters walk calmly, possessed of purpose and determination instead of fear and calculation. The people awake and serving coffee are happier than anybody drinking it, partly because it takes a certain kind of person to wake up at sunrise, and partly because that's better for the body clock anyway.

FIELD NOTES: FORGET IT, JAKE

Certain rules get dropped in favor of getting around or making a buck in Manhattan. If jaywalkers were vigorously prosecuted, the NYPD would make its budget in a day. Reddish-orange light-running is usually kosher as long as you aren't explicitly trying to kill a Jew. Peddling questionable goods wherever and whenever is usually a safe bet, though directly at odds with the commuting effort.

Chinatown turns this casual lawlessness up to eleven. Walking along the blurry and blurring borders of Little Italy and Chinatown is walking through a narrow bazaar of stacked clothing, buckets of trinkets, and crates of food. It's hard to tell what's being loaded into the stores and what's being sold on the spot. Sometimes it's being distributed to the street dealers: One crowd of peddlers gathered around a trash bag full of purses had a member whose job it was to fend off interested tourists with shouts of, "No sale! No sale!"

I recognized the shouter from the Starbucks team. She doesn't work at Starbucks, she works the sidewalk just outside. I assume she and the rest of her team recognize me by now, which is why I don't hear "watches, rings, watches, rings" muttered quietly in my ear as often as I did when I first started getting coffee there. As far as I can tell, they're selling approximately the same thing as the blocks of nearly identical stores selling knockoffs or otherwise acquired items, some in the window, some in the rooms you have to ask six or seven times to see.

The confusion caused by the masses of people trying to sell things on and off the street is roughly doubled by the hosts at the Italian restaurants trying to assure each passing tourist that the restaurant just to the left is the very best Italian restaurant out of the thirty or so that are holding up against the Chinatown onslaught. The only way to navigate or hold a conversation among the turmoil is to create a sensory blind spot and not give any indication that you can see or hear anything that isn't in the dead center of your vision. It's also important to do this for the sake of navigation, since the rules of right of way seem to be whoever got there first by not backing down. The roads tend to be 50 percent sidewalk, and there's often no way of knowing if that's because it's currently safe or if it just happens to be that way because some delivery guys took over a section of street, and will at any moment release a stack of angry traffic, or just run you down themselves with an overloaded hand trolley.

It's Chinatown.

APOCALYPSE

The survivors of an apocalypse—though this seems an odd phrase, no? The actual "end of the world" seems unlikely to leave survivors, except to punish in some non-euphemistically biblical sense. Maybe there's an early apocalypse phase, which would really make the remaining humans preapocalyptic survivors. Point is, a "postapocalyptic story" seems like a non sequitur; if it apocalypted, there's not much story to tell. Which is sort of the point: Just-preapocalyptic stories are about how to frame a story that will never be told.

In the nearly finished apocalypse, nobody cares who faced death with dignity. Nobody will be comforted by a brave face because nobody will be left to see it.

Veteran commuters will do well in this scenario. Long past the need to be understood or existentially validated, they merely need to be somewhere else, which is always an excellent place to be in any stage of an apocalypse. While the cinematically minded survivors are figuring out how to balance the need for sustenance with an optimally poetic death scene, the master commuter will still be trying to get somewhere in an efficient manner. That there may be no meaningful place to go is irrelevant: The commuter's goal is to move, and in the ultimate scene of a species' narrative, its last motion is its final meaning.

THE WEAVE AND THE KNOT

Spontaneous situational awareness achieves its most impressive demonstration at busy street corners during light changes.

A dozen paths from as many directions intersect over nine square meters of concrete. Eyes dart, calculating and recalculating velocity, step position, umbrella height, and baggage wheels. Miraculously, twelve strangers versed in the ways of the commute will converge in this manner and flow through one another without breaking stride.

There is the occasional hitch, and a commute of any significant length will doubtlessly encounter at least one. But though many focus on the errors and missteps that wear the soul down over the course of urban habitation, it's worth pausing to admire the awesome skill of the weavers at the corners.

Unless you're standing at the corner in question. If you pause then, you'll just fuck it up, creating a knot.

Any sailor or bondage enthusiast will rightly claim many knots contain beauty, but a knot by its nature does not contain motion, and thus is anathema to the commute. A weave become knot is a legion of frustrated intents, a mass of tangled headphone wires rubbed apart at great length and annoyance because of a single bad decision.

In the mean city streets, be a weaver, not a sailor.

FAILURE

Not all commutes are successful. The train will not enter the tunnel. The bridge is closed. The engine dies. Those who have never been late or absent ride the edges of probability even as they attribute their perfect attendance to mythical skills. The rest face the current of fate aware of human limits.

The consequences of a failed commute can be dire. A job may be lost—lives may be lost. A vital moment in a career, a meeting missed, a shift uncovered—all could change the course of a life for better or for worse.

The character of the commuter is revealed in facing such failure. It need not be the destruction of an ego built on a mountain of perfect commutes. It need not even be the ruination of a day, though many a sociopathic employer may attempt to make it so.

The struggle of the commute emphasizes the most-known potential consequences. All the elements of the story are understood: the self, the employer, the employment, and the means of binding them together. Failure in such circumstances is to fail at the entire endeavor of constructing identity in society. Thus it is here the commuter—the person—is truly tested. The known repercussions are the blunt instruments applied to the sense of self; the submission to chance obstruction on the well-traveled path is the subtler knife. It can undo a mind's defenses, and once shorn, it must choose between collapse and adaptation. To adapt is to accept that, even in the commute, the moment is like all other moments: the constant journey from the perfectly known to the perfectly unknown.

FIELD NOTES: STOP

There is a stop sign. There had to be a stop sign. It was too long ago, in a place I don't go anymore, where Orchard begins and Canal ends, in a little twist of neighborhoods competing for identity. The accidental cul-de-sac of near-death at the edge of Chinatown nullifies traffic laws even more than Chinatown Classic. It's a labyrinth of aggressive intent and stubborn persistence, with nary a traffic light to guide the way.

But there had to be a stop sign. There was always a stop sign. The delivery trucks and lost tourists always stopped at this god-forgotten corner. There had to be a stop sign because it made sense in my barely caffeinated mind to claim dominance over the T intersection between me and my subway stop.

The calculation seemed in my favor, but the calculation was skewed: Legally, it's always on the pedestrian side. Less so medically. But they had a stop sign, because if they had a stop sign, I could have retired off the lawsuit. They were a truck, of the cinematically boring sort: too small to host a fight on the roof, too big to make a handbrake turn. They wanted to go through the same intersection I did.

I walked as if I knew they would stop, because I knew they had a stop sign. They drove as if they knew I would stop, because they didn't see the stop sign. They followed the bumper of someone who slowed enough to pass a lie-detector test in California, but now it was my turn, so I walked. But they kept coming.

Evidence notwithstanding, entitlement does have its limits. The uncinematic truck had the weight advantage. I had to stop, about a foot away from my opponent's tire. The passenger gave me exactly the look I give to people who dig through their backpacks in front of turnstiles: a slight widening of the eyes, a half gesture of the hand, because a full gesture would grant too great a dignity to the idiot stranger. The unseen driver yanks the wheel toward me once they're halfway past, cutting eleven inches off the distance between me and the side of the truck, and forcing me to take a step back to avoid breaking my foot under the rear tire.

The fantasy writes itself: First, I am twice as strong as I am in reality. This gives me an edge in the inevitable fight against the condescending passenger and the unseen driver, at least one of whom is twice my size. It also makes it easier to rip the rearview mirror off the side of the truck and use it to smash the passenger-side window.

The shade-throwing passenger, once he's over the shock, makes a move to defend himself, but I grab his throat, pin him to the dashboard and say, "I don't want you," as I let my eyes drift to the driver. The driver either wets his pants or screams, "The fuck is wrong with you! Get the fuck off my truck you—Jesus!" as his passenger is ejected through the front windshield.

"I want you." Now he definitely wets his pants.

The rest is just angles and delays on the punches. A thirty-degree descending open palm to the middle of the jaw. A right-angle elbow strike to the cheekbone. A few upward knees to the solar plexus. Maybe a thumb in the eye. Because there had to be a stop sign.

SNOCALYPSE

No city is truly capable of dealing with more than four inches of snow. Many think they are. All of them are incorrect. There simply isn't anywhere to put it until it assumes its less-impolite liquid form. It gathers itself in haphazard piles and spreads itself in slippery plasma, all while collecting—and exhibiting—evidence of poor urban hygiene in diverse palettes of gray.

A city copes by clearing its airport runways and enough of its roads to maintain the steady flow of goods and bankers, and this keeps the city relevant enough for its host country to pay attention if too many people die during the cold snaps.

The only true differences between cities are in how their people address the inconveniences of snow accumulation.

Cities frequently assaulted by this base meteorological insult collect a population inured to the difficulties. Their citizens are prepared as if for pioneer times, coated in long johns and flannel and down, every resident knowing in their chilled bones that polite society will not protect them from a wrathful sky. They are prepared for the wilderness, because when the wilderness comes from above there is no escape, no matter the height of the concrete.

Where snow barely falls, city denizens are rightfully fearful. Even the best-funded snow responses of polar-adjacent cities are clearing the way for survivalists; what hope does an equatorial budget have against weaponized water unleashed on a warmhearted people? They close the hatches and keep their children away from the ice, because the cold is bitter and full of terrors. In these places, this is the responsible response, since the cold only mounts brief incursions to remind the warm that entropy is inevitable, and even the bitterest winds will fade come a fortnight at most.

In both extremes, there are those deficient in fear and preparedness: The young will ever test the suspensions of their pickups on icy roads and icy rivers, and die for their inability to recognize the supremacy of nature.

But the middle places are where humanity is tested, because the middle places are neither sufficiently prepared nor sufficiently afraid as a matter of policy. Mocked from the poles and the equator, temperate cities develop a complex, despite managing a range of temperatures dangerous at both ends. In the winter, this displays itself as insufficient winter wear atop impractical boots trampling through periodic patches of unshoveled snow outside storefronts of ambiguous liability. Interacting even less than usual as they hunch against the cold, and possessed of that most resilient of fashion trends, they become the Black Walkers.

When the snow accumulates more than an inch every two hours, it is incorrectly referred to as a "snowpocalypse." The proper term is of course snocalypse (SNAH-ka-lips), from the Greek snakalyptein, meaning "It's not, like, bad bad, but I don't think I'm going to work today." During the snocalypse, the inhabitants of the temperate city find their rat trails walled off in unpredictable ways. Normally traversable street corners are suddenly separated from the road by four-foot walls of ice and grit, forcing commuters to turn around and backtrack to another corner with an exit.

As many paths become single-lane affairs, the character of temperate city folk is revealed, for they are, above all, an efficient people. Given a ten-foot stretch of snowbound, single-lane sidewalk, first to an opening crosses, while the other waits. No discussion or planning is required: A year of undirected city living suffices to create this habit. The only communication needed between the two Black Walkers is a brief meeting of gazes to confirm the existence of a lingering spark of humanity in the Other that will prevent them from being a Jerk.

PLENTY

"There's plenty of room!" is a cry universally emitted by persons who do not expect physical violence. They may be of a disposition such that local social norms would frown upon a superior opponent visiting violence upon them. They may be of a proportion such that they do not fear altercation. They may be insane.

Whatever the reason, to those inclined to comment on the available space in a given compartment, this must be said: There is never enough room. There is certainly not "plenty of room" at any moment you feel the urge to claim the contrary. You will be accommodated with indifferent grace if there is in fact enough room for you, and you will make your way with humility. If you simply insist on declaring the impossible with the expectation that it will become true, you will one day encounter someone just like you. When that day comes, you will quickly discover how much room there is. Plentiful, it is not.

RAGE FANTASY

I have wished a great deal of pain upon strangers. I cannot vouch for the health of this mental habit, but I do believe it puts me in a thickly populated demographic.

My personal neurosis comes from a long-lost time during which great violence would have had little legal consequence, as long as it was conservatively applied and of arguable incitement. I never applied it, and even as the tempters of my youth found themselves universally at the mercy of officers of the state, I cannot shake the effects of their behavior on my psyche. I apply my unfulfilled hatred of them upon their unimprisoned counterparts, who continue to elbow their way through the crowds of people with too much to lose.

There are arguments implying that the behavior of those who decline clear offers of potentially justified violence are enabling. These arguments are always presented by those of violent temperament, who rarely if ever decline such offers, but let us consider the argument apart from its source.

A person who inflicts minor violence for immediate personal gain is perhaps ill-versed in the local etiquette, and the argument for confrontation claims that they must be trained or beaten into submission. When faced with the fact that this methodology inevitably fails, the fallback argument is that the person has led an insufficiently difficult life, and more difficulty must be placed on it.

Yet this fallback argument cannot truthfully be separated from the arguer, for it is inseparable from the ideological framework that emerges from suffering. To wit: I have suffered thusly; I adhere to my current set of mores; my mores are superior because they have superseded mores that were lost to suffering; the application of the suffering I endured will create better behavior when applied to others.

This is not a flawed argument in and of itself until you step back and consider a society full of people who think suffering is good and they should inflict it on another, which is most of the societies we have now. Perhaps it was inevitably passed down from times when suffering was inevitable, and death a daily foe instead of the desperately abstracted future it can be for the very few living in comfortable means and under sixty years of age.

The difficulty of living leads one to glorify the path that leads to each successive moment. I am as guilty as anyone of taking pride in my suffering, and in the restraint I show when faced with nemesis paths, even though they lead to constant rage fantasies. When in public, they consume my attention in a dangerous way, because they cannot be enacted within the framework of suffering I consider right, which involves not taking out my insecurities on others, so the rage uses all of my resources to eat itself into oblivion. When in private, my PlayStation controllers take the brunt of its expression.

COMPLEXITY

As systems grow more complex, order breaks down. The potential for error increases along with the cost of repair once the error is made apparent. Beyond its immense complexity, a city is a corollary to biological needs applied to geographical and technological constraint, and thus grows with exactly the predictability exhibited in the changing desires of its inhabitants, i.e., none.

This is all well known. Also known, but rarely admitted or examined with an appropriate degree of honest introspection, is humanity's vast overestimation of its ability to cope with complex systems. Indeed, far from admitting this shortcoming, they make torturous arguments to the contrary, most of which boil down to saying they weren't ready to invent the last thing they invented. This utterly nonsensical argument follows from the common and equally nonsensical argument that we have outdated brains that can't exist properly in the modern age built by those very brains. This line of reasoning might be valid if there were more than one data point; it will be worth dusting off if we run into a civilization like our own with different brains. As it is, the argument is barely worth filing.

The problem has never been that progress has gotten away from us; the problem is always that we think it hasn't. Alone or legion, we believe we understand the mechanisms of our day, and we never, ever do.

A city's public transit system is a concrete example of this: It cannot cope with its own success. Workers collect organically at the changing margins between the means of production and affordable living spaces. Public transportation mechanisms attempt to efficiently connect these temporary situations with permanent solutions. Once built, the margins rearrange themselves around the new means of transport, almost instantly rendering them insufficient. The margins push away again, even as the population increases at all points, new denizens attracted by new means of traveling to distant jobs. A "successful" city operates just beyond its actual capacity to support its population, which inevitably degrades its infrastructure. A city is fueled by a promise it ultimately cannot keep.

It is a situation that cannot be solved yet must be solved, and exists only because people cling to the notion that it can be solved because they think they understand the complex and destructive systems they create.

This is illustrated far more eloquently in John Carpenter's masterwork of commuting philosophy, *The Thing*. The thing itself is humanity's greatest achievement—adaptability—taken to its logical extreme, and applied to the desire to be somewhere else. It is a species, a complex system of transportation solutions, and a commuter all in one: a pure distillation of the operations of necessary movement. Naturally, it has to be killed with fire.

SIMPLIFICATION

It has been said of the philosophy of commuting that it should be compiled into a more digestible form. In lieu of a seemingly endless series of commentaries and notes, why not distill it into a few laws and instructions? It is certainly within the core principles to hold efficiency in high esteem, and not waste the time of any traveler.

Paradoxically, this pursuit of maximum efficiency in the most common journey cannot be reduced. Commonalities can be found, general principles can be ascertained, but the governing laws cannot be writ in metaphorical stone. What simple instruction applies to the transcontinental truck driver and the Bostonian exotic dancer? Be mindful of fluid intake, perhaps, but little else of importance.

The principles may be simple, but many who discover principles are quick to confuse them with applications. To discover a common principle is the first lesson. To apply it is the work of a lifetime. To confuse the discovery with that lifetime is the business model of Medium.com, and discernibly not the business of the serious commuter.

All select a core set of principles, and they are as random as an honest gambler's dice. Life's long task is to adapt those principles to survive the complexity of the next billion choices, and discover the unteachable adaptations demanded by the doors of serenity. Any thorough philosophy of lasting note is a temporary place of coherence that extends into complexity. To pretend it is a stable bedrock upon which to rest an understanding of the universe is to start a cult.

FIELD NOTES: NOBODY'S GOING TO DO ANYTHING

The man on the floor has, as a near statistical certainty, seen better days. He is sound of neither mind nor body, and looks to have aged more by circumstance than the passage of days. He kicks and growls more like a dreaming wolf than a human.

He is sleeping in the middle of the subway car. I had missed the telltale absence of torsos in the middle windows of the car, which during rush hour signals either a situation like this, or an abundance of evidence that it has recently occurred.

Still, having missed the signs, I take my place against the door and out of arm's reach, and commence reading.

"Is somebody going to do something?" wafts from the near end of the car. The content of the words identifies the speaker as a tourist with more certainty than the English accent in which they are delivered. No, you idiot, nobody's going to do anything. It's three stops to the river and the sleeping wolf has as much right to get home as we do. For that matter, this may be his home, and nobody likes to be bothered when they're sleeping off a mean drunk.

I glance toward the speaker. Very tall. Very large. Middle-aged. One of those soft-faced smiles worn by people used to picking up other people for fun. Damn. A righteous ogre.

I'm not the only city native to have noticed. His arm falters for a moment under fifty angry stares above fifty clenched jaws. But righteousness only hardens before challenge, and a meaty finger hits the button.

"What's the problem?" crackles the conductor.

"There's a sick passenger here," rumbles the ogre.

"Goddammit!"

"You fucking idiot."

"Fucking tourists."

The muttered curses and insults stream past the man and out the door as hundreds of passengers leave to nurse a drink until the traffic clears up. A cynical part of me wonders if he works for a bar.

CONTACT

The tenseness of fear is difficult to distinguish from the intensity of focus. For this reason are the new and lost oft confused for the old and impatient. The tension is shared and constant, at once providing common experience and obscuring that very commonality, as is tension's wont.

The eternal grind is born of this tension, but the situation also provides unlimited possibility for the serendipitous encounter. Most conscious contact, achieved when two or more commuters swim to the surface of tension's cruel ocean, is as deferentially delightful as the end of a Shakespearian comedy. The lined and rigid faces of hardened commuters ignite with concentrated kindness at the hint of someone asking for directions. The oblivious and the aggressive seem dominant only through the volume of misery they cause. Scratch at the doors of mercy and a far more powerful force will answer: the patience of masters balancing action and inaction for the good of the many.

Those who seek attention through disruption are easily identified and mistaken for representations of the places they infest. Look instead to the character of those who go quietly. They are eager to make a connection, and even more eager to practice the art of helping a stranger, for they worry the skill atrophies amid those who no longer need help, and those who cannot be helped.

ENVIRONMENTS

In the countryside, the land is the hindrance, and the people a source of aid when uncaged nature catches the scent of the unwary. In the city, there is no uncaged nature. The land is designed, however poorly, to aid the commuter, and it is the people who get in the way.

Even putting the commute aside, those suited to the navigation of nature will be at home in rural environs, while those suited to the navigation of people will find their skills daily engaged in a city.

Yet, in all environs, the most important navigation is of the self. The sufferance of the snowy hill between empty horizons, or the sudden crowd of French disembarking a tour bus, are challenges that will wither an uncharted soul. When the sea within is unknown, the obstacles of the outside world cannot be placed within a story of purpose. They are therefore overcome without reward, the very success merely adding additional chains of grudge and resentment. A well-mapped internal world allows the soul to anchor each day by islands of meaning. There it authors the story it means to tell, and buries its victories as treasures, to be someday unearthed in the remembrance of a rich life.

REVERSE COMMUTE

It is a peculiar characteristic of some organizations of commercial and residential districts that certain flows of commuters are nearly monodirectional. A given path, often a river crossing, all but bursts with bodies heading to a concentration of offices in the morning, then bursts again in the other direction at the day's end.

When employment and residence require travel symmetrically against this tide, it is referred to by all as a reverse commute. No literal interpretation of the phrase makes a great deal of sense, but it does convey the notion of going in a direction so contrary it no longer qualifies as simply a commute, and must be given a linguistic qualifier. One is no longer default: One is reversed.

The reverse commute presents a slightly different set of advantages and disadvantages. For instance, an individual obligated to travel from Manhattan to Hoboken at nine in the morning will find themselves privy to all-but-private cars on the PATH train. On the other hand, they will be equally alone at transfer points, forced to creep along the edges of corridors and wait beside stairwells until the overwhelming horde of commuters going the proper direction are done with them.

As set apart in language, so set apart in life. The veracity of suffering is determined by the silent vote of commonality, and assumed perception of small advantage is the lock on the door closed to the unrelatable suffering of others.

FIELD NOTES: TRAIN ONTOLOGY

The first month I was in New York City, I was trying to go home from a concert, because I was young and that's what young people do in the city between midnight and one in the morning.

I was waiting for a G train, on the G train track, when a train with a bright blue C pulled into a station that, to my knowledge, only entertained faded green G trains. I turned to a stranger and asked, "Is this a G train pretending to be a C train?"

He scowled at me and replied, "It's a C train pretending to be a G train."

No pairing of claim and counterclaim has occupied my mind as thoroughly and for as long as this one, except perhaps for the cross-when-you-have-to versus cross-when-you-can debate.

Succinctly, is a train its route or its designation? Since the train took me through all the stops a G train would usually take me, and dropped me off at the one I wanted to go to, it was as much a G train as any G train ever trained, all the while sporting its bright C, so it was G train pretending to be a C train.

Or, yanked from its native rails, it was forced down unfamiliar tracks, to compensate for G train failure, a temporary change before it returned to its day job, so it was a C train pretending to be a G train.

G trains are infamous for their inability to fill a station, as they're a few cars short of an average train, so had I known this and been paying attention at the time, I could have judged its physical attributes and concluded it was a C train pretending to be a G train.

All new trains' identities are displayed digitally. Length will be a demarcation for the G train until it's not. The physical signage demarcating a train's identity will fade faster. With no time to change each marker of a train's identity, it was once possible to know a train was not on its normal track. Now with a flip of a switch, a train is only its serial destinations, with no meaningful history beyond a passenger's entry and exit.

AUTONOMY

There is a scale of personal control along which all means of commuting lie. At one end is walking, wherein the commuter's means of enacting intentionality is restricted only by the means of their body and the laws of physics and local society.

Cycling is a minor concession of freedoms, especially when the cyclists ignore the laws of society and are limited only by their often unwise momentums. Less patience is given to cars, but along the open road many a choice remains, even if personal position is confined to fiddling with seat adjustments. Buses and subways further restrict path and velocity, only slightly less than ferries (though exceptional swimmers have many more freedoms on ferries).

At the far end of the scale is the commercial airplane. Once the initial decision is adhered to long enough for the wheels to leave the ground, the commuter's fate is out of their hands in an acutely conscious way.

Greater speed comes with a proportionate loss of control over the immediate future of the body. It is not statistical ignorance that drives—so to speak—people to prefer the automobile to the plane. It is the loss of control: the true and terrifying knowledge that their fate is not in their hands.

Yet the deeper fear is of knowing too well that our fate is never in our hands. Though a bitter draft, air travel, along with its ancillary humiliations, is a moment when this willfully ignored truth cannot be denied. Thus, it is a moment to test our ability to acquaint ourselves with the knowledge that all our vanities are indeed in vain.

TIME DILATION

As time and space are measured by the speed of light, subjective experience of time is measured by the length of one cigarette. A cigarette takes five subjective minutes. The speed of light can say whatever it likes; the hard edge of consciousness measures a smoking interval from the intent to smoke to the return to the nonsmoking world as a five-minute interval.

A watch measuring the personal experience of physical traversal through the fourth dimension will never agree with this measurement. It does not matter if the cigarette is consumed over a drink on a summer's day in three watch-minutes: The cigarette is five mind-minutes. Ten minutes to put on a jacket, take an elevator down, smoke, and take the elevator back to the office? Five minutes. Hastily sucked down in subzero temperatures outside a Norwegian bar? Five minutes.

This can be a boon in both the workday and the commute. If five subjective minutes can pass ten to fifteen watch-minutes, a day can be shortened by an hour or more. A pleasant block in a commute can be stretched with a vigorously sucked cigarette, while the experience of a boring quarter-mile slog can be cut in half with a cigarette gently tended.

Be wary of intent retardation. The greater the standard time between intent and the lighting of the cigarette, the shorter and less satisfying the cigarette will be when measured in mind-time: Given a four-minute delay between intent and lighting, even the most languidly consumed Marlboro will rarely be attended to for more than seventy-two mental seconds. A common experience is disembarking a train only to be trapped behind a slow-moving stairwell mob, whose thirty-second delay will be experienced as a three-minute march preceding two watch-minutes of anger-smoking. Experienced smokers may alleviate—at the risk of exacerbating—some of these effects by opting for American Spirits, which consume thirty subjective minutes.

Nonsmokers of course have their own subjective experiences of time, but, alas, no yardstick with which to apply mathematical rigor to their suffering and relief.

Maximizing speed is not a foundational principle of commuting, for good reason: It is dangerous. Indeed, the pursuit of speed conflicts with the core principles. It inherently creates friction, invites conflict, and the necessary increase in attention paid to the path directly ahead precludes proper consideration of potentially more efficient routes.

Some armchair scholars have argued that the principle of shortest path encourages similar dangerous navigation, and this is true in theory. In practice, however, even the novice practitioner will note that, though the shortest route from a tenth-floor office is through the window, such means of travel will not result in an optimal commute. Slightly less mortally threatening shortcuts are often taken by those pursuing speed, and though such commuters are adhering to the language of shortest path, they endanger themselves and others with their misaligned values.

Speed should never be pursued as end in itself. Rather, it should be seen as a positive effect arising from proper execution of legitimate fundamentals.

The principle of least friction guides us in such circumstances and allows us to follow the lesser way. The lesser way does not maximize our speed, nor is it even the objectively shorter path. Yet it is necessary for smooth execution of vital maneuvers, such as the zipper and the weave. The lesser way is the small sacrifice of time for the benefit of all. It is also, ultimately, for the benefit of the self, as brief moments of humility are the balm for the unnecessary indignities inflicted by a frustrated desire. The golden practitioner accepts this truth, and knows it is better to fail together than succeed alone.

FIELD NOTES: ASSHOLE VS. YOGA BUSINESS

"Dude, don't touch me."

Everybody hates this person. He broke the rule. He brought attention to the fact that all of our scared and lonely brains occupy twitchy bodies that are crammed against other twitchy bodies twice a day, all for want of a paycheck and a place to watch Netflix. We try to ignore him.

The poor bastard next to the hated man is in classic subway yoga form, and fully suited and tied despite the heat. He responds, at his own risk, "Sorry, man, it's just crowded."

The Asshole enacts a delicate dance of earbud rearrangement, and replies, "Yeah, well, look, just don't fucking touch me."

Yoga Business swallows deserved anger, rolls his eyes, and tries to stay upright.

Another stop. Some depart, some arrive. Bodies are jostled in the rush-hour press. Yoga Business presents the ten contortions that allow the impossible press of bodies to move to their resting states. Earbud Asshole retorts: "Dude, you gotta step away from me, I'm serious."

Yoga Business, bent around six other people and attempting not to fondle a single one of them by accident, has had enough. "Man, fuck you. It's crowded."

"Yeah, well . . ." (searches for a brain cell) ". . . just don't fucking touch me."

Why does this person live in the city? Or use public transportation? How does he not know that the armpit of the world is occasionally literal? And why is he leaning against the pole if he's so fucking concerned about personal space?

The stops continue. The comments continue. I yearn for a terrorist attack so I can save Yoga and leave Asshole to die. You're breaking my argument, Asshole. You're the person who makes everyone worse. You're the person who makes people crave firearms. Four billion years of evolution has presented you with a brain that navigates a world of infinite possibility, and you decide to be a basic bitch. Take the next step, you fucking worm. Give me an excuse.

And he did.

Because when patient Yoga Business arrived at his stop, Asshole turned around and threw a punch so poorly planned and embarrassingly executed you wanted to pat him on the head and give him a speech about how practice makes perfect but maybe he should take up chess. Even so, history's saddest punch still hit Yoga and gave him the much-sought-after Perfect Excuse he needed to break Asshole's face.

But I was bigger than them, and I needed to get to work. I shouted, "Yo, YO!" and put a hand on each of their chests, pushing them apart. I gave an extra shove to Asshole, to make him feel small, and to make him feel like he was shoved against a subway door twice.

I followed Yoga through the river of people, but couldn't get close enough to him and couldn't figure out how to best communicate "I'm sorry to have interfered, and you were right. That guy was an asshole, and you should have had the opportunity to beat him senseless, but I was just trying to streamline the human flow so we could all get away from him."

I followed him as I tried to compose a more efficient sentence, but his commuting was superior to mine, and he slipped away.

I noticed later that I was wearing a T-shirt that said DISTURBANCE CONTROL TEAM.

TIME AND MONEY

"Time is money" is the insistent shriek of hardening souls, an urge to efficiency in the transmutation of the most unchanging and ever-diminishing resource into that most fungible expression of faith in global institutions.

Time is infamously not fungible. An amount is portioned to each mortal sentience and drained away at a relatively constant rate. All too aware of this, humanity has set itself to the task of its best use. This has informed the entire infrastructure of modern commuting, along with every complaint about its failures. The slow commute brings the tension of this relationship to the fore, mounting at each moment spent without profit.

The unexpectedly aborted commute teaches much about this disordered thinking. High-earning employees can simply return home to sort things out at a later time, and often do so with relief, unless they have been sufficiently Stockholmed. Poorer workers, suffering under the bonds of replaceability and disrespect, must struggle or beg their way through the delay and to their next paycheck. In this sense, money is time: Its accumulation allows great freedoms in the future use of time, both via the fallacious concept that the fact of its accumulation should allow the accumulator greater freedom, and via its ability to buy the services of others in lieu of engaging in particular tasks at one's own temporal expense.

These notions lead to the mistaken impression that money can reclaim time already spent. The truth to ponder in gridlock or train traffic is that time's consumption varies greatly in the subjective experience of its quality and rate.

The "well" in "time well spent" is a value judgment, and the context of the statement should be paid a wary attention. It is an openly suppressed secret that the persistent conversion of time into money is not the best experience of time consumption, and all that can be done with that money is moderately improve the experience of the time remaining. Calculate this transaction carefully, for that remaining time is often less in amount—and harder to improve—than it appears.

FAST LANES

Roadways have clear lanes for various travel speeds. They are not always respected, but they are marked and known.

Walkways generally have hazier demarcations, creating much of the strain involved in using them. Their lanes are more like canyon winds, disturbed by eddies, unpredictable and ephemeral. The fast lanes in foot traffic consist of the paths few want to follow, and few want to follow them because they are dangerous.

The edge of a subway platform is the most famous of these, and the most commonly used by people sure of balance and sparse of enemy. It is also the lane most often blocked by the oblivious, requiring dips into the common lanes as often as not.

The edge of the sidewalk, behind vendors and hydrants, is a narrower path, closed to many, and requiring a tenuous truce with the bike lanes. The bike lanes are a no-man's-land, marked as such seemingly to attract delivery carts, cars, pedestrians, and—worst of all—cyclists.

Last and most ubiquitous, though rarely recognized as fast lanes, are sidewalk grates. Barred to most in high-heeled footwear, and irrationally feared by many others, grates are often the passing lanes of experienced walkers.

STANDING ON THE TRAIN

Some must sit on a train, and many even desire it. However, given a workday entirely comprised of sitting in a chair, added to the possibility that you may not notice a pregnant woman in need of the seat you are not giving her, one may opt to stand. Given a nonpacked train, there are several options.

At the exit door is optimal for an experienced train commuter, and failing that, being near the door will allow for a relatively speedy exit, particularly when exiting at an unpopular station. Both of these increase entry and exit efficiency, but incur a greater certainty of jostling and irritation, and require closer attention to the movements of other passengers.

To avoid dealing with it altogether, obtain a central position between two doors. This is often looked on as a sacrifice, and the position will be given consideration above and beyond the mathematical advantage that people will move away from this position more than they will move toward it.

An even better standing position to settle in for a long leg of a commute is against one of the doors that lead between the subway cars. They can be identified by the signs on them that read RIDING OR MOVING BETWEEN CARS IS PROHIBITED just above the DO NOT LEAN ON DOOR signs. Once the body is leaned on the door and an appropriately bracing foot position is established, the only concern is the people moving between cars, who are few, though generally aggressive and unpleasant. The downside is being all but trapped when attempting to exit through people who are not leaving, and are in fact backing toward this position as the greater exodus emits from the center positions.

There is no ideal place to stand. All are forms of compromise, but compromise is an inevitable consequence of motion in a gravity well, for all beings who grasp the concept.

FIELD NOTES: FULTON STREET

If you need to kill someone, do it in the Manhattan Fulton Street subway station. "Cavernous warren" means little outside fantasy novels, except at Fulton Street. Transfers are crowded mazes composed of narrow passages low of ceiling and bare of bulb, until they empty into vast halls of ramps for wheelchair-bound ogres. The halls absorb many tributaries, and be wary of thinking an upstream journey along one of them will release you: Endless construction, barely scheduled and never advertised, blocks more than one exit. The rumble of trains loses its connotation of anxious plunging into unknown darkness; in the halls of Fulton, it is the pure promise of escape.

The design of the Fulton stop calls into question the entire enterprise of civilization. If this lies at the end of our most monumental efforts, what was the point? Why continue? For here is the evidence that all our struggle for order can never escape the creeping decay that confounds our every attempt to ease the burden of mortality.

If you need to kill someone, do it in the Fulton warren, because the body will never be found, and they may even thank you for freeing them from the purposeless joke of existence.

At two minutes, eyes begin to roll, but it's nothing out of the ordinary. A recording announces train traffic or a signal malfunction or a sick passenger. Nobody knows if it's true. Most are beyond caring.

At five minutes, watches and phones are furtively glanced at. The time is marked: The delay will be storied, and judged.

Fifteen minutes sees a surge in activity as people attempt to send apology texts to coworkers and loved ones. This awakens the sleepers not already stirred by the interruption of the comforting rumble of progress.

Twenty-five minutes begins to strip away the armor of commuting personalities. Some strike up conversation, seeking humor and companionship in the face of horror. Elsewhere, knuckles begin to pale. Teeth begin to sing frustration and helplessness.

At forty minutes, silence falls, as the human soul understands that if there is a God, He has turned away.

After an hour, the screaming begins. The screaming begins, and will not stop. On the other side of the car, glistening eyes watch a hand rest gently on a window, a supplication to move the world.

INTOXICATION

There is a fundamental feature of all cities with twenty-four-hour public transportation: They are drunker. There is never a need to drive home. There is never a need to ponder the cost of a taxi, or the need to explain where one lives to a taxi driver. There is only a need to not throw up in public, but that has never stopped anybody from throwing up in public.

The twenty-four-hour transportation is everybody's pumpkin carriage, always ready to carry the inebriated far enough away from public victories to leave them unmarred by private degradations. By simple statistical inevitability, misfortune strikes most in the home and the workplace, but there's often greater risk in the paths between them, and worse decisions made.

Take a hypothetical personage getting, as they say, "blotto" at a strange bar with a dermatologist whose name, phonetically to a Western ear, is literally "win win." Will this hypothetical person, almost as drunk on perceived luck as he is on actual alcohol, immediately buy the pack of cigarettes he was moments ago claiming he would never need, to celebrate? He shall. Were this person chained to an automobile of no small collision insurance, would he have driven home feeling six inches taller than he was? He would have. Did he? No. Because he didn't own a car, and the spiral of poor choices available to every drunk person terminated at the nicotine habit that turned his second date into a lose-lose. He instead took the public transportation, still running at an acceptable capacity at two in the morning.

It is perhaps arguable that our hypothetical idiot would have practiced a degree of moderation had he known there were stricter legal impositions on his means of transport. But let us bask in knowing that he had no further opportunity to misuse his autonomy, and could only clutch a wall in a tunnel full of machines made to take him home.

AWARENESS

There is no debate about the optimal level of awareness in self-guided automotive commuting: as awake as possible short of acute amphetamine psychosis.

For walking and public transport commutes, there is a wide range of methodologies. Long train rides and short flights offer the option of actual unconsciousness, though a particular kind of indentured capitalist chooses to work over these periods.

In less extreme examples, it is possible to effectively commute in states from near-sleepwalking to highly caffeinated. On a long-traveled commute, this becomes a matter of preference, as the various eccentricities of the path can be navigated by rote. Anything requiring attentive awareness would have to be so out of the ordinary it would activate the necessary attention automatically.

Still, there is an argument to be made for maintaining heightened awareness even in the deepest rut of an old commute, as few situations are so frictionless they cannot be smoothed, and it is the duty of the practitioner to both hone and apply the skill of their discipline.

For the master commuter, there is no difference between commuter and commute. Thus the master is simply aware of the master, and need no longer address the question.

FIELD NOTES: DOG

The lack of agency in subway commuting is not a privilege to be scoffed at. As a young man in Maine, I commuted with the car, a crass, unsubtle instrument that allows for little ambiguity in announcements of sick passengers and path obstructions. If somebody between my origin and my destination had to be taken to the hospital, there was little doubt whose name would show up on the court docket.

I never hit a human on my many commutes between home and schools and restaurants full of customers who couldn't tip and waitresses who hated their husbands. But one morning, I woke up late and didn't have time for coffee and climbed into my car and sped off through the rural road to the other rural road to the rural road that called itself a route because it passed a gas station.

On the first rural road, a young dog made a break for the other side and hit my bumper instead.

I remember seeing the human on the side of the road running and screaming, taking attention away from the furry blur, a little like a person screaming, "Watch out!" so the person under the piano will inevitably look to their unmaker. It wouldn't have mattered even if I could trust my memory so long after. The car was moving at thirty miles an hour, forty-four feet per second. I saw the furry blur ten feet in front of me. With an average human reaction time of .25 seconds, a foot too late, at best.

I stomped on the brakes and laid two twenty-foot tracks of burnt evidence in the road in case I tried to forget before the next paving. I was stopped at this point, and still late.

I got out of my car and walked back to the mother of the stunned children, who were still processing the notion of violent, personal death, maybe for the first time. The mother was holding the dog, still alive, with its head turned all the way around, no longer able to bark, nerves severed, eyes still looking at me, moments away from death, shocked and disabled, asking who is this new person? Why can't I move my feet? Why can't I open my mouth? What just happened?

"I'm so sorry," was all I could say, trying to meet the mother's eyes, trying to tear them away from the dog's.

"You couldn't have avoided it," she said. I don't think I could have. But I could have been to work on time. I could have made coffee. I could have forgotten to fill the gas tank yesterday. I could have done some tiny thing differently in my whole life and prevented this exact moment from happening. The always true and always useless knowledge of hindsight has a way of sticking in the brain when you've done something you cannot undo, even if you already know you can never undo what you've done.

"Is there anything I can do?" I asked, uselessly.

"No. But thank you for stopping." And putting some face on a killer, or some faithful and shared suffering on a death. A human with regrets is better than a license plate vanishing behind a trail of blood and screaming children. That's why war movies have plots between slaughters.

The cost of being a being a flawed and decent human is bearing the weight of the pain a human must inevitably create, and it is better to leave the navigation of heavy and fast-moving metal to others whenever possible.

BLADDER

There are no restrooms in the New York subway. Once the subway is visited, it does not require any peculiar mental exertion to imagine why. Even the public restrooms protected by private and sometimes armed enterprises map a matrix of antisocial contempt for the public. To use one is to stiffen the lip and pray for better social services, superior ethical character, a hand sanitizer that does not itself require sanitizing, and, perchance to dream, the elimination of teenagers.

But the small mercy of not encountering subterranean hellholes is little comfort when desperation would cherish any kind of hole for turning bodily waste into someone else's problem. Youth simply suffers under these conditions: The imbibing of social grease glitters too bright and blinds foresight, leaving the young bladders fit to burst anew with each delay. The incautious among them have been known to brave the dark territory between train cars, and some have perished.

Sadly, there is no recourse, and as experience blunts the need for more experience, the aged refrain from excessive drink until they near a trusted toilet. The master never asks the student to practice this abstinence, for she knows it is a trade ultimately made with relief.

STAR COMMUTE

It is taken as read that the navigation to the stars will be a militant traversal modeled upon Earthbound navies. Admirals, not generals, rule space.

In most ways, a star force would be more similar to an air force, in every technology and consideration. But air forces came long after land and sea forces, and long after titular distinctions were important in the economics of war. The generals can have the air in the modern era, because nobody cares anymore.

Space feels like the sea in its lingering brutality. The sky is taken briefly and gloriously, the oceans navigated at length and peril. Space is never taken: No journey is quick, and all are made in lonely vessels, thinly separated from the unforgiving medium they traverse.

Yet for all the poetry shared between space and sea, the cold hardness of air travel is the board on which the interstellar commuter plays. Realism-oriented science fiction necessarily includes among its central plots the consumption of energy. All travel has specific mathematical bounds: A ship can go this fast, support life this long, slow down this much, and never get too close to the fusion balls.

The emptiness of space neatly boils the commute down to its meanest components. A mind and its proteins burning fuel in a little world, alone and praying the physics are right.

The dangers and limitations of space travel are much the same as life, but distilled and romanticized in a situation where uncomfortable questions are brushed under the rug of impending death. The real and fictional explorations of space ask, "How do we live?" and gift moral gratification for simply continuing to do so. In this, it is the opposite of war, the exploration of which asks, "Why did we die?" and never provides an unburdened answer.

It might do the human species well to see its wars as taking place on a spaceship that provides a delicate afterthought of a life-support system during its stately commute around a star we barely know.

DARTING

For all their planning, patience, composure, and poise, every commuter will one day see an opening, a moment when a sudden rush through an unexpected clear path becomes almost rational and too tempting by far. The window of opportunity is too brief to properly calculate all the variables. These moments exist at the edge of consciousness by definition: They can only be exploited before thought. The motion required to navigate them is referred to as the dart.

Dangerous by nature and abused by the unwise, there is no communal patience for the dart. Even executed perfectly, it is frowned upon. It may ripple disruption in its wake no matter its precision. For these reasons it should never be attempted.

But it will be, by all, sometimes successfully, sometimes disastrously, and sometimes fatally. Since prohibition has, historically speaking, never worked, anywhere, for anything, education is required to reduce fatalities.

The dart should only be attempted while moving; sudden motion from a standing position all but promises collision. Furthermore, though it bursts into the commuter's awareness, opportunities should only be taken from a place of maximum possible awareness of the surrounding situation. Acting without context is the mechanism of dramatic irony, and the outcome of a poorly executed dart will be no less dramatic or ironic.

Be it a slippery stairwell or an unseen car, a sudden yet banal death is the risk on the scales opposite the reward of arriving at a destination ten seconds sooner. It would do well to hold that knowledge close to the forefront of the decision-making process, such as it is. Yet, for all that, if the decision is made, there can be no hesitation, and may a god smile that day.

FIELD NOTES: TRAVEL BLIND

Before I had an iPhone, some people stopped me while I was walking to the train and asked me how to get to Skillman Avenue. I looked around, uncertain, then shrugged apologetically and told them I couldn't help them.

On the way home that day, I happened to glance up at the street signs and found Skillman Avenue. It was exactly one block from where I'd had that morning's encounter. I had crossed it thirty seconds before saying I didn't know where it was. In fact, I'd crossed it twice a day for two years.

I bring this up because there's a school of thought that suggests my familiarity with my route should make me sensitive to any change, but in truth, I never get that familiar with any of my routes. In a new route, I usually navigate by address the first time, then by landmark, but within a week, I'm going by muscle memory. The landmarks I no longer need are the only things that still grab my attention, since the repetitive locating I did the first week burned various mantras in my head like "turn at the church" and "bear right at the gas station." Everything else in those first few walks was categorized as "not the church" and "not the gas station." Once I know a route, I switch on autopilot and spend the walk thinking about coffee and what to do once I get out of work.

So it shouldn't be surprising that I don't notice things like buildings going up or falling down along my route. Unless something actively blocks my path or makes enough noise to annoy me, I'm either checking for traffic or not really there at all.

I'm not even sure if the gas station is Sunoco or Shell. Damned if I know the denomination of the church.

DRAFTING AND SLICING

Most of the tactical skills in commuting are only applied in middle-density traffic. Too little traffic, and a simple acknowledgment of the broad strokes of commuting theory will suffice. Too much, and no tactical application will help, and it is better to find contentment in meditations upon the philosophy.

However, the bulk of average commutes exist in the middling tactical space, and there are two indispensable tools every commuter should be ready to apply. Though described here from the perspective of walking, drivers will find them applicable with only mild tweaking of the measurements.

Upon spying a fellow commuter traveling at optimal speed, it is acceptable to begin drafting them. The drafted commuter finds the path, circumvents obstacles with the necessary apologies and expletives, gauges the flow of oncoming traffic, and manages the expectations of that traffic's constituents. The better part of necessary situational awareness is handled by the draftee, and the drafter only has to maintain an invisible connection to them, signaling subtly to others that drafter and draftee comprise a single commuting unit. Optimal drafting distance is approximately six feet: close enough to signal unity, far enough to not be weird.

Slicing is a means of guaranteeing optional lateral movement, without taking attention from forward motion. It consists of passing oncoming persons or groups of persons with the smallest amount of interceding distance. Once done, it is practically certain that the space on the side the pass is made will not contain an overtaking pedestrian, and the commuter is free to move in that direction without checking. Slicing generally provides a three-second window, but, of course, if the move is desired, it is best done with all expediency.

EMOTIONAL MANAGEMENT

There will be times when the commuter is trapped in a small space with someone demanding a response. It may be a mystery what that response is. There may be no adequate response. The response may not be in the category of responses the commuter is willing to give. Yet the demands continue.

Aggression tends to increase as the response is not given. Silence works sometimes; other times, it is the worst tactic. The demanding party may take a half-hearted acknowledgment; they may not. They may not be able to recognize the response if it is given. They may not accept the response unless it is extracted via a particular means, or given in a complex, even ritualistic manner known only to them.

The demanding party has focused on some aspect of another person that qualifies that person to act in this call-and-response interaction. The demander is so invested in their desire, they mistake it for need, and inevitably work this need into a comprehensive worldview in which they deserve to receive their desired response when they call for it.

When faced with such a person, and the required response cannot be given, all that can be done is to carefully gauge the demander's emotional temperature and calibrate responses to keep them manageable until escape is possible. No set strategy is known; it must be determined and applied in the moment.

This advice, of course, is meant for men, who refer to this situation as "being trapped in a small space with a crazy person." Women refer to it as "going outside."

ENTROPY

The master commuter aspires to minimize the entropy produced by the commute, according to the principle of minimal friction. A mastered commute consumes little energy, producing the smallest possible amount of heat in the body and its surroundings. It requires little exertion, and avoids anger and anxiety: cool of body, cool of spirit.

Low entropy is also low information. A well-executed commute all but vanishes in the mind, as the mind engages only in response to new information, or, as it is better known, local increases in entropy.

Here there are considerations not informed by the principles of commuting. The well-executed commute still consumes time, and if that time slips through the mind without imprint, it is time unexperienced, unremembered, and lost without benefit to the soul.

To master the commute is to master a necessary expenditure of time. The commuter seeks to reduce this imposition to its smallest negative effect. Yet one should remember the time is still spent, however efficiently. If the time is merely lost due to the sublimation of the process to unconscious automation, it is still a loss, no matter the elegance of the achievement.

To be human is to take pride in the clever circumvention of hardship and indignity. Mastering this cleverness always risks sacrificing the experience of being alive to the task of mastery. Thus the lesson, taught by all true masters, is to introduce a modicum of entropy, pain, and indulgence, so as to not forget the path traveled.

HEAT

Blacktop sends up waves and the withering air waves back. Squint and the walls melt. Doors blast air to freeze the sweat against your skin. You exhale, inhale, one, two breaths of relief before the fog of heat drapes back over your shoulders. You shiver as if cold, wonder if your body is broken, trying anything to fight the heat.

Words struggle out of your throat, your brain is melting, can't direct attention or parse sentences, try to maintain footsteps to shelter, left, right, left, right, shuffling, dragging, everything is wet and clinging.

—It's not the heat, it's the humility.

Old joke, half a smile. Wipe the sweat out of your eyes. Buy a soda. Descend, down, down.

The fans kick the dust and nothing else. Dripping bodies slide past one another. Everything is . . . moist. Moist rolls off the tongue moistly. The word sounds like what it is, spat out, hissed out, a bastard word that wanted to be so many other things but ended up moist. Your socks are moist. Your skin is moist, coated in soot, your shirt is moist, sticky, sticking, finding new ways to bunch and wad around your body.

—Dude, fuck you.

Emotion at volume cuts through the haze, but don't do it, please don't do it, you just want to move, slide slickly between the doors, just a few more feet, just one more connection, just get me out of this, don't fight in the heat, don't stop the motion, just go it's not worth it he's not worth it.

Staggering now. One more stop in a refrigerated coffee shop, a bodega with water, water! One more sip of water and free air-conditioning, you can make it, you can make it, two more streets, two more white rock ovens and steaming grates. Where is the water coming from?

—Why is it so wet?

Concrete spires shimmer above steel mazes; where does all the steam come from? The air in front of you is so thick you try to part it with your hands, but they do nothing, there's nothing you can do. The sun fills half the sky and sends its reflecting demons to every window, so many windows around you, there is no shade, no shade, no shade, you seek every shadow, beg for the water to rise into cloud, there's never enough shade, never enough shade.

—It's like a goddamn swamp.

But it's not swamp water it's piss water, it's desperation water, it's want water sad water never-tried-hard-enough water bored water crazy water late water Jesus-where-did-this-water-come-from water. Water that hates itself as much as it hates you.

You reach a door. Maybe there's a job behind it. Maybe an interview. Maybe water that doesn't hate you. It doesn't matter. It's shelter. There's something else behind the door. Get through it. Get away from the hateful star. Go through it. Go.

FIELD NOTES: CONTRARIANS AT THE GATE

Every day that I've come home at rush hour for the last seven years, someone has pushed open the emergency exit gate. At first I thought these people were just trying to be cool and contrary, as in, "Yo, cat, I'm a New Yorker, these rules don't apply to me," but once my blood turned to coffee and the last of my nerves were shredded and I actually became a New Yorker, I realized it's for the best. Several hundred people get out at my stop, and stuffing them all through three turnstiles is like getting wet salt out of an Applebee's shaker. Another hole can't hurt.

Though I often go through the opened gate, I never open it, as that would violate the principle of least effort. It takes slightly more effort to open the gate than to push a turnstile, and no effort at all to walk through an open gate, so strict application of this principle dictates always walking through an open gate, and always opting for the turnstile if nobody else has opened it. It also sets off an alarm that I could live without.

After a few more years, I started going for the turnstile even if the gate was open. Most people shoot for the gate, because the gate tends to be a faster exit, and this is in line with the equally important principle of fastest commute. But at a critical mass of commuters, this stops being true, precisely because enough people think it is true, so you have a trickle of commuters flying through the turnstiles, and a thick line shuffling through the gate. Furthermore, people are coming at the gate from two angles, and though it appears the gate can handle two people going through at once, this never happens due to the alarming space-consumption-to-body-size ratio most New York commuters display, so you get microsecond delays whenever two people make for the gate and discover this. This double bottleneck slows the gate exit to a degree at which, even if the gate is strictly closer to the point where I exit the train, I can skip a line of thirty people to go through a comparatively untouched turnstile.

Even with a firm grasp of the principles of commuting, context and commuter density must always be factored into calculating the net benefit of applied tactics.

ALL IS REAL

Few activities in life anchor the soul to objective reality more securely than commuting. However high one may elevate the practice of its principles, it remains an expenditure of time across space in pursuit of sustenance in the service of a system with few escapes. The human soul will never extinguish the yearning to put the time spent on a commute to better use, nor should it.

Yet this forced engagement with the real does much to prune frivolous thinking from the mind, as well as provide the potential to grasp the complex connectedness between thought and form.

The more fanciful theories of ontology die quickly, and badly. A brain waiting behind a stoplight waits, be it in a body, a jar, or the depths of space. No essential oil or self-knowledge will repair a signal malfunction. The commute is solely a physical transaction, its hardships and victories solely physical.

But let us not be reductive. Etiquette and mood are discussed as ethereal concepts but are no less real than a door in their effects on the experience of the commute. A mutating line divides discourse into the real and the conceptual, even as physics and mathematics dance an aggressive tango atop the towers of academia. The most energy-efficient commute is navigated amid atoms, hormones, and theories, interactions subtle and overt, as complex as all the motions of every conception of heaven. The changing heart, the adaptive mind, the inclement weather, and the battle between union and state share practical value with the energy grid and brake maintenance. All is the movement of energy, told in a story that might move another's heart, and all is real.

DOOR POSITION

Among the more coveted spaces on a train are the spaces in front of the doors. There are two such spaces, one on each side of a given doorway. Technically, a third space exists in the middle, but it is a difficult space requiring constant movement, and is often quickly lost. In the two good spaces, a commuter can lean comfortably, freeing up both hands, and if it is on the side of the train they will have to exit, it guarantees an unobstructed and rapid egress.

It is not a space for the novice train commuter, for it requires a delicate etiquette. Everybody wants the space, so the stander must prepare the heart to accept a minimal level of envy and hatred directed against them. To manage this for the good of all, they must be aware of both the incoming and outgoing traffic. It is necessary to exit the train at major stations—notably Union Square, Atlantic Avenue, and Grand Central—in order to make way for the mass exodus that invariably occurs. Worse, the space must be vacated given a critical mass of incoming commuters. If it is possible to quickly and accurately count the number of incoming passengers, the post may be kept, or reassumed after stepping outside to release outgoing passengers. If the number is higher, or, for the visually minded, if empty space cannot be seen between the future copassengers, it is necessary to migrate into the center of the train, or, if possible, the other door.

To do less is to impede the ability of others to follow the principle of least resistance, thus it is verboten to assume the door position without full awareness and strict adherence to its laws.

SENSES

Optimal commuting requires all the human senses. Smell, touch, and taste have their places, but we prefer not to speak of them, so let us skip to the most obvious: sight, for those blessed with it. It is a perplexing feature of the human condition that many so blessed choose not to use this most trusted sense. This lays the onus of its effective use upon the master commuter, who must see what others are not seeing.

However, trust in sight is misplaced: The eyes doth indeed deceive with some frequency. The brain, no fool, thus made hearing its foremost warning system. An eye accepts both lie and error, forcing its patchy perception into continuity for the sake of convenience and suppression of nausea. The ear is not in such a hurry to force its assumptions on the world, and pricks up at the slightest discontinuity that might suggest danger. The eye guides us through the day, but the ear protects us from the night.

(This, among myriad other reasons, is why the compassionate traveler does not snap gum next to their fellows' ears. One might as soon turn on a strobe light in a bus, or slowly shove a needle into the back of a child's neck. It is an assault, made all the worse by its pointlessness. It is the aggressive twitch born of a child's desperate need to be noticed, a strangely acceptable variation of petulance, a prolonged form of whining that balances maximum effect and plausible deniability.)

Properly trained, the ear can do much more, serving as the proverbial "eyes in the back of the head," providing a rough spatial map of activity otherwise out of sight.

At this point it might feel alarming to recall how many commuters are staring at screens and wearing headphones. As distressing as these people are, the death rate remains remarkably low, because even with all-but-shuttered eyes and ears, most commuters have a powerful tool that is rarely even acknowledged as a sense: proprioception, or the sense of one's own body. Proprioception is so vital that its loss renders the mammal nonfunctional, and so powerful it can move a body through most of a complex commute with a dash of memory and an occasional glimpse of the environment. As many as do die, behind or in front of the vehicular wheel, the miracle that we don't all die in such circumstance can be attributed to the ability of proprioception to extend itself and merge with rolling steel combustion.

It is not a panacea, however, so please stop texting.

A regular commute will involve regular beggars. What the nonhomeless try to think of are the subway performers, the luckiest of whom peak at becoming warning signs: Their performance reduced and shrined in bathroom-sign cartoon figures, to wag the encouraging finger at future generations of extroverted athletes.

Sadly, these are not the only people asking for money. Some beggars are fleeting. Most will seem fleeting because you won't see them every day: Their schedules are optimized to a different set of factors than the average salaryman. Ass in a chair, ostensibly working; hands on wheel, obviously working: These workers present a visible, taxable demonstration of time exchanged for money. They are recognized and recorded. Beggars spend invisible hours as waiters of virtue signaling. They rely on a squishy gray space between the ability to game human empathy and actual empathy.

Most homed commuters cobble together a moral argument to avoid giving their loose change to the homeless, usually along the lines of, "You don't know what they'll do with it," and there's no denying that the kids on the train are certainly not raising money for their after-school programs, and that a certain individual on the L train who needs "bus fare" every morning and afternoon is an asshole. The argument falls apart somewhat in the face of burn victims who have extreme difficulty operating in normal circumstances because nobody wants to look at them.

Nobody wants to look at any of them, especially the ones seen week after week on the same streets with the same stories. So we—I—look away. There's no moral argument. There never was. I can't help everyone reaching out to me and pleading for help. I want to, because I am not a monster. But I can't, so I act as a monster would, trying to give the impression that I am not aware of the existence of the person holding out their hand, asking for anything at all. Secretly, I watch all the other people who walk by them doing the same thing.

Psychological horror stories sometimes feature a punishment that never fails to chill the soul: a person sentenced to never be acknowledged by others; not exiled, but forced to move through the world as if they do not exist. Millions execute that exact sentence every day on the people with the least means of escaping it.

When I do stop to give money or a cigarette, or even talk, I often see release in their eyes. Not for the physical things I give them, but small, simple relief at being recognized, a taste of the social glue that reminds us that we do exist in a world of other people who exist. The evidence that people like me have not yet completely exorcised their humanity, having deemed it too great an imposition on our morning walks.

RIGHT OF WAY

On the seas, right of way is a simple set of rules. Faster vessels give way to slower vessels. In a head-on approach, both vessels veer starboard. Upwind gives way to downwind, port to starboard.

The laws of the land are less clear, perhaps due to the lack of wet and salty doom beyond their failure. The closest land laws come to maritime is the order of operation at four-way stops. There is an unearned faith in the ability of land creatures to navigate one another effectively, even as they gaze in awe at the ability of sea and sky creatures to navigate an entire extra dimension, en masse, with a grace to shame the Russian ballet.

In some ways, natural etiquette rises to meet codified standards: fast gives way to slow, lanes are weakly adhered to, cars attempt, mostly, to not hit pedestrians.

But landlubbers travel without respect for their medium, taking for granted the hard ground upon which they tread. This leads to arrogance and inattentiveness, so it is best to remain aware even when the patchy laws of land are favorable. Nobody wants "they had the right of way" on their tombstone.

FIELD NOTES: SHAME

Once, many years ago, I dropped my coffee in the subway. The explosion: instant. The wavering blob of caffeine and cream spreading out under my feet, guided by petulant opposition to the motion of the train: eternal.

"Oh, damn," was all I said when it happened. For a moment, I thought I could stem the flow of the blob and my shame with my shoes, but it was pointless. Soon it was spread into a thin sugary film at which thousands of strangers could shake their head, after it ceased to be my problem. Not long after that, it would be a discoloration still more thousands of strangers would try to avoid identifying, and then, some hour or day away, it would be eliminated by soap or upstaged by urine.

I could only hang my head and wait for my stop.

Relieving my embarrassment somewhat was a victim of the initial explosion. An errant arc of morning courage had ended its trajectory near the cuff of his pant leg. He huffed and gave me a glare. Then he swore and fished a napkin from his pocket, which he used to make exaggerated sweeping and scrubbing motions on his pant leg, interspersed with more swearing and glaring.

I could not take umbrage at this aggressive shaming dance, because I had sinned under both the letter and spirit of subway law by bringing my coffee in the first place, and further demonstrating the reason for the prohibition of precariously sealed fluids in inescapable public spaces. It wasn't umbrage I wished to take, however; I merely wished to ask him what he hoped to achieve. I could not undo the action, nor could I assist him in fixing it. He merely wanted to make me feel worse, according to the theory that the emotional account of his life would be better balanced if his displeasure were more publicly known.

I was reminded of this today when I stepped on a woman's foot. It was crowded. Another woman had to leave, and my pole yoga was weak that morning, so as she pushed by me, I stumbled back one inch too far. I felt soft resistance on my back heel and knew it was being resisted by poorly protected flesh, so I turned and said, "Sorry." The stepped-upon woman rolled her eyes at me and went through a series of sighs and expressions to demonstrate her lack of patience with my faux pas.

I'm ill-equipped to respond to this form of social negotiation. They want to make me feel worse on their terms, to cut me on the edges of their passive-aggressive weapons, to ensure pain in case I'm insufficiently socialized to regret having accidentally harmed them. Since I do feel reflexive regret, I feel the social debt is paid, and resent the assumption that I need to be trained like a child unaware of its transgressions. They succeed in making me feel worse because I find their efforts so offensive, but to respond to them would simply feed the loop of each party needing the other to feel the worst—if only by an inch—at the end of the encounter.

To protect its story of its place in the world, the human defaults to escalating accusation. As I have demonstrated in the preceding words, I am not above this, but it is better to refrain from inflicting one's needs on others prior to reflection.

HOMEWARD

The first step out of the last door in the building is the most vigorous of the day. The brain begins filing the big problems into the subconscious to make room for the necessary route planning. Once planned, lingering emotional baggage is transmogrified into lust for drinks and/or companionship. This is kind of a problem: Suppressing angst of all sorts tends to push toward pondering potentials, so work becomes longing for home and home is marred by dreading work. But in the transitional spaces the emotions are palpable and engaged in the now.

On a busy street, freedom is indeed slavery, and optimism burns quickly as the fuel needed to reach the first choke point. The subway entrance is always crowded. It is always crowded even if the subway is not running, as the people who have given up and are making their way back out to find alternate trains are rarely sure enough of the situation to accurately give warning to the next people who may or may not see a train arrive. In addition, the people exiting under such circumstances are extremely angry, and not predisposed to help their fellows.

Assuming the train is running, there is a trudge to the optimal car for future exit, which is always blocked by at least one exceptionally slow-moving person walking in the middle of the platform with several bags. They may be young, they may be old, their bags may simply be other people who think it is acceptable to completely block a walkway so they can continue to complain about work and friends. They may be hunched over a cell phone. They are all very terrible people, for whom no sigh or *tsk* should be spared.

Optimal position achieved, there is a moment of stillness, to recharge the spent optimism. Perhaps a book is unpacked and opened. Perhaps a phone game is played. Regardless, the recharge is expedited by the brief relaxation, and takes exactly five minutes, at which point it begins decaying with a half-life of ninety seconds until the train arrives.

The twin strainers empty into one another. There are two antagonists in this process: the one who attempts to board before the current passengers have disembarked, and the one who forgets they're disembarking until the new passengers have boarded. Odds of encountering either of these beings is one in three, making one in nine transitions especially difficult.

Once on the train, a period of sporadic rest occurs, where the mood only improves slightly as the exit point approaches, since the stops in between cause the human particles to jostle and annoy one another, raising the temperature both metaphorically and literally.

If there are any transfers, repeat paragraphs three through six for each transfer.

Eventually, the last stop. The mood soars, or at least improves, depending on how many people between you and the train door exist and aren't leaving. Hatred for these penultimate obstacles swells disproportionately to the excitement for whatever awaits on the surface, but subsides into an almost gentle and always condescending annoyance during the final walk to the exits. The stairs can be taken slowly. There is no more pain. A flickering fluorescent begins to give way to sunlight reflecting off grubby steps. Glance up. There, a hint of sky. Relief.

Unless it's winter.
Then it's dark.
And cold.

NIGHT AND DAY

There is no substantive difference between commutes to and from work. Roughly the same number of people at each station, roughly the same chance of subway catastrophes, and the dour half-awake expressions of pre- and mid-coffee morning travelers are difficult to distinguish from the exhausted and drained slouches of the evening passengers. The evidence of personality is as crushed by semi-consciousness as it is by a fully realized workday.

The cosmetic differences are seasonal. The end-of-day subway exodus in the summer is the moment the pace of the day finally slows. In the winter, this doesn't happen until people get to their homes and bars. The environmental oppression is roughly equal between seasons; the exhaustion caused by hurrying through the cold creates the same physical muting as the in-tunnel summer heat that simply robs the body of the ability to move.

As often as not, the last obstacle after exiting the subway is a long traffic signal. Most of the time, the commuters cluster at the corner and peer down the streets, hoping for the rare break in traffic during the endless DON'T WALK light. They look past one another in much the way they walked past one another ten hours earlier, when they weren't ready to communicate, now not bothering because they have nothing left to say.

A commute defines more than a path of daily travel. The polar destinations define the bulk of experience: the restaurants, the bars, the Seamless options, the parking, etc. The route itself is the experience oft first remarked upon to the inhabitants of either destination, thus the qualia of the commute and its subsequent social dissemination is defining of the commuter's initial character at both office and home.

It is a small slice of the whole of a personality, but it is a slice, and it will radically change with any change of job or home, or means or path of transit between the two. The commute is a circuit, and viewed over a lifetime it can be stable or wild, the heat plate of a coffeemaker or the lightning of a storm. Its variance will both imply and inform the character of its traveler.

QUALITY

A commute is an endlessly repetitive journey to rarely changed destinations. Folk wisdom about the comparative values of journeys and destinations wear thin under such conditions. Yet they hold a lesson as important to the commute as it is to any other activity: The answer to the question, "Will this be worth it in the end?" is "No."

The metaphorical elegance of the commute is that it poses, with great regularity, the far more important question, "Is this worth it right now?" Great life choices and changes, with all their turmoil, are often made with the tentative belief that there may be an end that will balance the initial disruption. Yet such upheavals tend to occur when the now becomes literally unbearable, and it must be literal, as there is no ceiling in the tower of complaints that will never change a nearly unbearable present.

No matter the quality of its end points, most commutes test the bearability of the now. It is an excellent moment to ponder the balance of needs and desires and where the satisfaction of each has left the quality of life. On the commute, the barrier between internal aspiration and objective progress is at its thinnest, and one may find revelation after being trapped under a river for twenty minutes.

Cities grow, and bring hard hands to build spaces for soft-handed laborers. All migrate to dense metropolises to suffer cramped public transportation to even denser urban areas, whereupon they don headphones and communicate by email.

For some, it is a bitter trade required by the employing elite following increasingly questionable principles of productivity and socialization. These workers view the city as a series of indignities to be suffered stoically in the pursuit of riches. Those of such opinion, whether they come to the beckoning cities or not, think of the urban middle class as a herd of drones being ground between the gears of commerce.

Though not entirely wrong, those who think this way do not last long. Statistically, an average of three years, after which they break or flee, leaving the rest a measure of relative peace.

The survivors need the indignities of the city to keep them moving. Whatever the work, it is the puzzle and punishment of the city that engages. What is a banal and modest chore elsewhere becomes a daily achievement worthy of song in a city, and once the unending tribulations are, if not mastered, efficiently navigated, the rewards of a city that is not Boston stretch well beyond any meaningful attempt to consume them. Pain awakens the senses to paradise.

Those who go to live in hard places to work rarely finish a lease. Those who work in hard places to live never leave.